DATE			

First Aid for Backpackers and Campers

First Aid for Backpackers and Campers

A PRACTICAL GUIDE TO OUTDOOR EMERGENCIES

LOWELL J. THOMAS
JOY L. SANDERSON

ILLUSTRATED BY KATHLEEN SANDERSON

HOLT, RINEHART AND WINSTON
New York

Published simultaneously in Canada by Holt, Rinehart and Winston of Canada, Limited.

Library of Congress Cataloging in Publication Data

Thomas, Lowell J.
    First aid for backpackers and campers.

    Includes index.
    1. Backpacking—Accidents and injuries. 2. Camping—
Accidents and injuries. 3. Hiking—Accidents and injuries.
4. First aid in illness and injury.
I. Sanderson, Joy L., joint author. II. Title.
RC88.9.H55F57   614.8'77   77-21297
ISBN Hardbound 0-03-021106-9
ISBN Paperback 0-03-021111-5

First Edition

Designer: Helene Berinsky
Printed in the United States of America
10 9 8 7 6 5 4 3 2 1

Acknowledgment is made to Eric Gold for technical assistance in herpetology.

To Our Camping Family

Contents

First Aid for Backpackers and Campers

Introduction:
Before You Go

Every day more people are seeking wilderness experiences. Many of these people will not have adequate knowledge of simple first-aid measures to handle an illness or emergency when there is no medical or paramedical assistance available. As college instructors teaching health, first aid, and nursing, we have had numerous queries from our students about how to handle emergency situations in the wilderness. First aid is the immediate and temporary care given to the victim by the rescuer after the injury has occurred. The key words are *immediate* and *temporary*. The rescuer must be able to provide quick and easy treatment, using available materials. When you are in an unfamiliar area, using improvised equipment, it is essential that you be able to react immediately, accurately, and without panic. We feel our book will assist you in these situations, since necessary information is organized for quick reference and the first-aid techniques can be quickly performed by following specific, step-by-step directions.

We have included subjects not usually found in first-aid texts because we have tried to foresee the special kinds of first-aid problems that arise in the wilderness, and to suggest procedures that are most likely to be effective until adequate medical help can be obtained. This book also differs from most first-aid books in that we assume backup medical or paramedical assistance is not readily available. The methods used have met with repeated success and are accepted by many medical sources. Although the book is indexed so that emergency information can be readily found, we urge you to read this book through before you begin your backpacking, camping, or vacation.

Our focus in the book is on wilderness first-aid problems, but similar emergencies can arise at home, at work, or at a picnic. The first-aid measures we suggest are applicable anywhere, so keep our book handy—in the car, office, kitchen, cabin, tent, or backpack.

To use the book in an emergency, locate the key word that best describes what has happened by using either the cross-referenced index or Chapter 7, "Common Emergencies." If the situation permits, before you start to treat the victim, quickly read through the entire procedure. Then follow the step-by-step directions and refer as necessary to the specific drawings for visual assistance in the treatment. We do want to stress the importance of being able to act automatically when you encounter airway obstruction, cardiac arrest, or hemorrhage, so we recommend you become familiar with these emergencies by carefully reading Chapter 1, "Wounds and Bleeding," and Chapter 3, "Choking, Respiratory, and Circulatory Emergencies," before you may need this information.

BEFORE YOU GO

We list below our suggestions for preparing for a safe trip. The suggestions are not in any order of priority or importance. Choose those most appropriate for your outing—whether you go on a one-day trip in the car or a two-week retreat to the back country.

- Read *First Aid for Backpackers and Campers.*
- Take a course in cardiopulmonary resuscitation (CPR) and first aid. The American Heart Association, American Red Cross, and most community colleges offer these courses. The skills learned in these courses are useful for everyone, whether practiced in isolated areas of the country or in the backyard. We urge all people— junior-high age and up—to undertake and complete courses in first aid and cardiopulmonary resuscitation.
- Take time for a complete physical examination. Discuss health problems and immunizations with your doctor. It is important to be protected against tetanus if you expect to spend time hiking and camping in isolated areas. Check with the Forest Service of the area you will be going into to see if there are any special immunizations needed; if you are going out of the country, check with the U.S. State Department. If you haven't had a recent dental examination, make a dental appointment. A throbbing, persistent toothache can ruin your vacation as thoroughly as any injury.
- Encourage members of your group who may need specific emergency treatments to wear Medic Alert tags or carry health-information cards. Medic Alert tags may be obtained from Medic Alert Foundation, Turlock, California 95380, and information about them is available from many pharmacists. The tags provide rescuers with information about any special medical needs should the person become unconscious or unable to speak. Examples of pre-existing medical conditions that may require a specific first-aid treatment are diabetes, epilepsy, and known severe allergic reactions to insect stings or penicillin. If you have one of these or any other potential first-aid need, it is wise planning to let others in the group know what to do for you in an emergency and to familiarize them with the special medications that may be required.
- When the trip is expected to be strenuous or if you have been inactive for some time, start early with conditioning activities and exercises. Bicycling is an excellent and

enjoyable way to build up strength in leg muscles and to increase lung capacity. Running or jogging may be what you prefer, but don't try to catch up in a few weeks for a winter of hibernation; start in plenty of time to increase your distances gradually. Carry a loaded backpack around the house and yard while you are working, or go on one-day hikes. Not only will it strengthen the back muscles you will be using, but you will get a feel for the weight distribution. You will also find out if any adjustments need to be made in the frame or straps. If your boots are new, break them in by wearing them for increasing lengths of time while carrying the pack.

- If you have never gone backpacking before, check into the adult-education or recreation departments in your town or at a local community college for course offerings. You can practice the skills of backpacking and learn what is available in equipment and supplies. There are also many good books in the library on these subjects.

- Planning for the trip should include learning all you can about the area into which you are going. By doing this, you will be better able to anticipate what type of clothing, foods, and equipment will meet your minimum needs. Inquire about climate, elevation, availability of water, and degree of difficulty of the trail. Also, by becoming familiar with the terrain and elevations by means of topographical maps, you can plan for the distance to be covered each day. It is the group leader's responsibility to be aware of the fatigue levels of the hikers and to stop before anyone is tired and consequently more likely to become ill or have an accident.

- Let someone know where you are going and when you plan to be back. The Forest Service requires trail permits in many areas, not only to prevent the overuse of the wilderness, but also to be able to alert their search-and-rescue personnel if backpackers don't return when expected.

- Lastly, learn where you can find help if injury or illness does occur and assistance is needed to get to a medical facility. When you register for trail use, ask the rangers for suggestions in summoning and/or finding help. They may have information about lumber or Forest Service camps, or about the location of private residences in the area. A plan for getting help in an emergency is just as important as a plan for evacuation of your home in case of fire.

The outdoors offers wonderful recreational experiences, and we hope you will enjoy them. We believe that this book and a properly equipped, lightweight first-aid kit (see Chapter 8 for list of items) should accompany you on every backpacking, camping, or vacation trip.

1

Wounds and Bleeding

Bleeding that is not severe is not of major concern to the backpacker. Each backpacker should know enough to wash his hands thoroughly, cleanse the wound, bandage it with a clean or sterile dressing, and then check for infection periodically. Our major concern is to acquaint you with the procedure to follow when a member of your backpacking party is wounded seriously and bleeds profusely.

Serious bleeding requires immediate care. If a large blood vessel is severed or lacerated, a person can bleed to death in one minute or less. When backpacking, the rescuer should know how to handle such a problem quickly, using available materials. When bleeding is severe, the following steps should be performed in order.

FIRST AID FOR SEVERE BLEEDING

Direct Pressure

Firm, steady, direct pressure is the simplest and most often effective method of controlling serious bleeding from most wounds. Direct pressure may be applied using a heavy, sterile gauze pad, dried seaweed, moss, or any clean material directly over the wound (Fig. 1-1). If a sterile or clean material is not available, place your hand directly over the wound and apply firm, steady, direct pressure (Fig. 1-2).

The direct pressure is to be maintained until the bleeding slows or stops. At this time you may bandage the wound snugly, keeping pressure over the bleeding site with a heavy gauze pad (see Specific Bandaging Techniques, in this chapter). If a blood clot forms over the wound, try not to disturb it. Once bleeding stops, clots will usually form within 1 to 10 minutes. You may apply the bandage over whatever material you used for pressure.

Elevation

If no fracture is present, a wound that is bleeding severely should be elevated. That is, the injured part of the body should be raised above the level of the victim's heart. Elevation uses the force of gravity to reduce the blood pressure in the injured area. If a bone is broken, see Chapter 5, "Bone and Muscle Injuries," for treatment.

Direct pressure should be continued while the extremity is elevated (Fig. 1-3).

METHODS OF APPLYING DIRECT PRESSURE

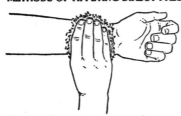

Fig. 1-1: Direct pressure with moss

Fig. 1-2: Direct pressure with hand

Fig. 1-3: Elevating while maintaining pressure

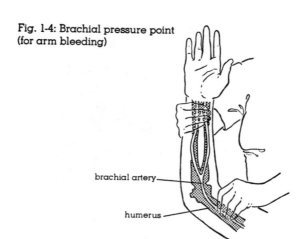

Fig. 1-4: Brachial pressure point
(for arm bleeding)

brachial artery

humerus

Pressure Points

If severe bleeding continues from an open wound on an arm or leg and direct pressure and elevation have not stopped the blood flow, the next step is to use the appropriate pressure point in combination with the direct pressure and elevation. The pressure-point technique temporarily compresses the main artery supplying blood to the extremity, reducing or stopping the blood flow. The two main pressure points are the brachial (arm) and the femoral (leg) arteries. To apply pressure to the pressure point, feel for and find the pulsating artery, then force the artery against the underlying bone. More than 90 percent of severe bleeding can be stopped with this type of pressure.

BRACHIAL ARTERY: Apply pressure to the brachial artery by forcing it against the humerus (the upper-arm bone). The pressure point is located on the inside of the arm in the groove between the biceps and the triceps, about midway between the armpit and the elbow. To apply pressure, grasp the middle of the victim's upper arm with your thumb on the outside of the arm and the other fingers inside (Fig. 1-4). Press your fingers toward the thumb, thereby forcing the brachial artery against the

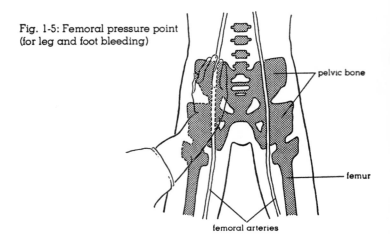

Fig. 1-5: Femoral pressure point
(for leg and foot bleeding)

pelvic bone

femur

femoral arteries

humerus, cutting off the blood flow below the pressure point.

FEMORAL ARTERY: Feel and find the pulsating femoral artery; then apply pressure by forcing the artery against the pelvic bone. The pressure point is located on the front center part of the leg in the crease of the groin area. To apply pressure to the femoral artery, position the victim flat on his back, if possible, and place the heel of your hand directly over the point where pressure is to be applied (Fig. 1-5). Keep your arm straight and lean forward to apply pressure. By keeping your arm straight and directly over the victim, you will prevent arm tension and muscular strain.

ADDITIONAL PRESSURE POINTS: In Figures 1-6 through 1-10, other pressure points are shown with their proper execution.

Tourniquet

A tourniquet is a band drawn tightly around a limb to arrest serious bleeding. The use of a tourniquet is rarely necessary, as most cases of bleeding can be controlled with a combination of direct pressure, elevation of a limb,

PRESSURE POINT AREAS

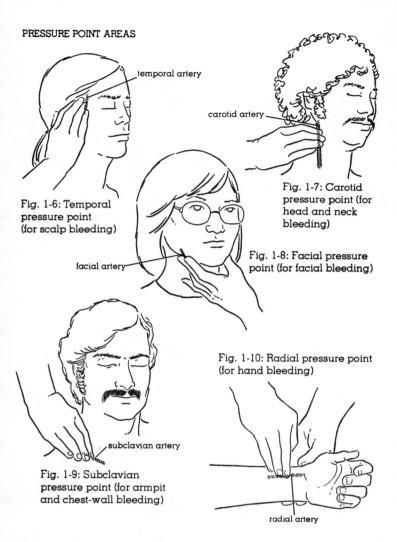

temporal artery

carotid artery

Fig. 1-6: Temporal pressure point (for scalp bleeding)

Fig. 1-7: Carotid pressure point (for head and neck bleeding)

facial artery

Fig. 1-8: Facial pressure point (for facial bleeding)

Fig. 1-10: Radial pressure point (for hand bleeding)

subclavian artery

Fig. 1-9: Subclavian pressure point (for armpit and chest-wall bleeding)

radial artery

pressure points, and firmly applied dressings. Tourniquets should be avoided whenever possible because of the danger of nerve and blood vessel damage and potential loss of limb, but there may be cases in which bleeding continues and a life may be lost without the use of a tour-

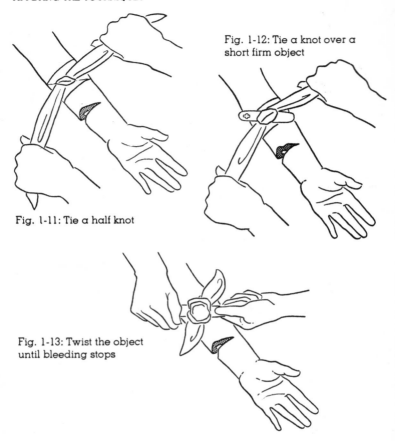

Fig. 1-12: Tie a knot over a short firm object

Fig. 1-11: Tie a half knot

Fig. 1-13: Twist the object until bleeding stops

niquet. The motto to remember is "life or limb," because after two hours of tourniquet application, the limb will be lost. If all other methods fail to stop serious bleeding, and you decide to place a tourniquet on the victim, do not allow it to be removed by anyone except qualified medical personnel who can treat for severe shock and can surgically control the bleeding.

The best tourniquet is a piece of strong cloth about 2 by 40 inches, but any material may be used. For example, a triangular bandage, a piece of shirt or pants, a bandanna, or a soft belt, approximately 40 inches long and 2 inches wide, would be adequate. You may have to tie several pieces of material together to make it long enough.

To apply a tourniquet:

1. Place a tourniquet just above the wound, but not on a joint; do not let the material come in contact with the wound.
2. Wrap the tourniquet band around the limb twice and tie a half knot (Fig. 1-11).
3. Place a short stick, branch, fishing-pole handle, closed knife, or similar object that will not break on top of the half knot and tie two additional overhand knots (Fig. 1-12).
4. Twist the object to tighten the tourniquet until the bleeding stops (Fig. 1-13).
5. Secure the stick in place by looping ends of tourniquet over the stick and tying a knot on the side of the limb opposite the stick.
6. Mark on the victim the time the tourniquet was applied.

Do not cover up the tourniquet with anything. It must remain visible so it can receive immediate attention when medical assistance is obtained.

BANDAGING TECHNIQUES AND THEIR APPLICATION

Basic Bandaging Procedure

1. Anchoring a bandage: Place the end of a bandage below the point of the dressing on the wound at a slight angle (Fig. 1-14). Encircle the part of the body so that the upper corner of the bandage end is visible (Fig. 1-15). Turn down the visible corner of the bandage (Fig. 1-16) and encircle the corner part again.
2. Covering the dressing: To cover the dressing on the

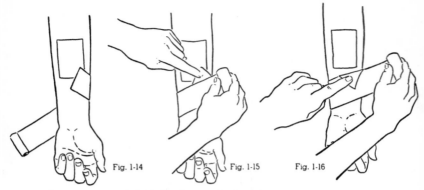

Fig. 1-14 through 1-16: Anchoring the bandage

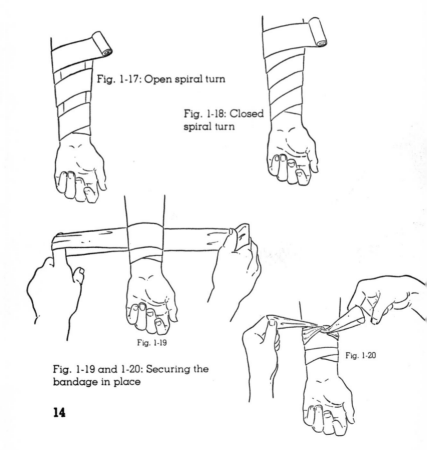

Fig. 1-17: Open spiral turn

Fig. 1-18: Closed spiral turn

Fig. 1-19

Fig. 1-20

Fig. 1-19 and 1-20: Securing the bandage in place

wound, you may either use the open (Fig. 1-17) or closed (Fig. 1-18) spiral turn.

3. Securing the bandage: If you have used a roll of gauze to cover the dressing, you can fasten it by bringing a loop of the gauze around your index finger (Fig. 1-19), then bringing the gauze ends up and over the dressing and tying a knot, avoiding the top of the wound (Fig. 1-20). If you do not have a roll of gauze, you can use any kind of tape or a safety pin, clip, belt, bandanna, or piece of clothing.

Specific Bandaging Procedures

FOR FOREHEAD OR SCALP WOUND: For forehead or scalp bleeding, use a triangular bandage, bandanna, or similar large piece of cloth. Fold to a triangle about 54 inches long at the base; then fold up long edge to provide a 2-inch wide band, 4 to 6 layers thick. Place a dressing directly over the wound and the folded edge of the triangular bandage above the eyebrows (Fig. 1-21). Secure the dressing and bandage in place by crossing the ends in back (Fig. 1-22) and wrapping around to the front to tie (Fig. 1-23). Finish off by tucking the point in back up over the cross (Fig. 1-24).

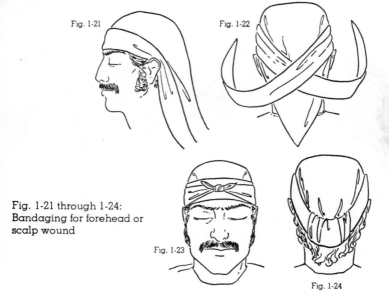

Fig. 1-21

Fig. 1-22

Fig. 1-23

Fig. 1-24

Fig. 1-21 through 1-24:
Bandaging for forehead or scalp wound

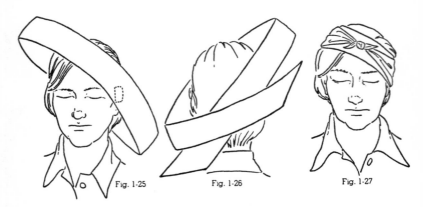

Fig. 1-25 through 1-27: Bandaging for forehead, ears, or eye wound

FOR FOREHEAD, EARS, OR EYE WOUND: Place the dressing directly over the wound, with the triangular bandage folded to 2 inches wide over the dressing and wrap around head, tying ends in front (Fig. 1-25 through 1-27).

FOR CHEEK OR EAR WOUND: Fold a triangular bandage to 2 inches wide; place over the dressing (Fig. 1-28). Cross the ends on the opposite side of the injury (Fig. 1-29), bring the ends around to the injured side, and tie in place, avoiding top of wound (Fig. 1-30).

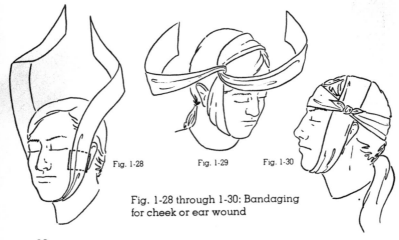

Fig. 1-28 through 1-30: Bandaging for cheek or ear wound

Never use these bandaging procedures for suspected jaw fractures or when there is bleeding in the mouth. The bandage will not allow blood or vomitus to drain out of the mouth and the victim's airway could be blocked.

FOR KNEE OR ELBOW WOUND: For a wound on the elbow or knee, bend the joint at a right angle unless the movement produces severe pain. Use a triangular bandage about 54" long folded to about 4" wide. Always begin with the middle of the bandage over the dressing at the knee (Fig. 1-31). Carry the ends around in the opposite direction with one end around the upper leg and the other around the lower leg (Fig. 1-32), crossing and securing them in place (Fig. 1-33). The procedure for an elbow injury is essentially the same.

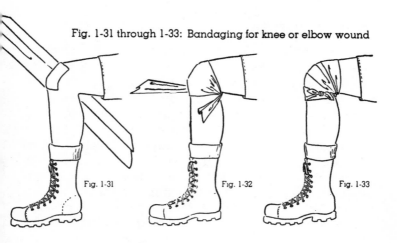

Fig. 1-31 through 1-33: Bandaging for knee or elbow wound

Fig. 1-31   Fig. 1-32   Fig. 1-33

FOR HAND OR WRIST WOUND: The figure-eight bandage is best used to stop bleeding in the hand or wrist. This can be achieved by anchoring the bandage at the wrist as in Fig. 1-14 through 1-16. The next step is to carry it diagonally across the palm and around the wrist as many times as necessary (Fig. 1-34). Complete by tying off as in

Fig. 1-34: Bandaging for hand or wrist wound

Fig. 1-19 and 1-20. This technique can also be adapted for an ankle injury.

PREVENTING CONTAMINATION AND INFECTION

Open wounds are subject to contamination and infection. The danger of infection can be lessened by taking the proper first-aid measures when treating severe bleeding, such as using clean or sterile dressings, cleansing the wound properly, and covering it to avoid outside contamination. Infection does not appear immediately but rather takes between two and seven days to develop. When backpacking, your immediate concern is to stop the bleeding with the cleanest material available and to begin your hike back to medical help where proper treatment of infection can take place. Since medical facilities may be some distance away, the injury should be checked en route for signs of infection. Some common signs of infection are tenderness, redness, warmth, and swelling. More advanced signs are pus, red streaks extending from the wound, fever, and headache.

If severe infection develops, it is extremely important that the *interim* first-aid steps be applied.

1. Keep the victim lying down and quiet if possible, immobilizing the entire infected area. This will de-

crease active blood flow in the infected area and slow the spread of infection.

2. Elevate the infected body part, if possible.
3. Apply heat to the area. This can be done with warm, moist towels or with hot rocks covered to prevent further injury. Local application of heat will reduce pain and help the body destroy bacteria.
4. Transport the victim to a medical facility using a method in Chapter 6, "Emergency Transportation," that is the most appropriate for the type of injury.

REMEMBER: The above steps are only a temporary treatment, and immediate medical help is necessary.

2

Shock

Shock is a nonspecific term referring to a state of generalized inadequate circulation. The most obvious cause is external hemorrhage, but it may develop when there is no visible blood loss. The body fluids are simply being redistributed in ways that make them unavailable to vital organs. The general rule to follow is the greater the injury the more likely shock will occur. In cases of serious injury, the priorities for treatment are:

1. Airway and breathing
2. Pulse and circulation
3. Severe bleeding
4. Poisoning
5. Shock
6. Fractures

The symptoms of shock vary depending upon the degree. Some of the symptoms are cool, moist skin, restlessness, apprehension, drowsiness, rapid shallow breathing, general body weakness, rapid and weak pulse, and finally, unconsciousness.

TREATMENT: Take care of life-threatening situations first, such as bleeding and breathing difficulties, then treat for shock.

1. **Body Position:** Elevate the legs about 12 inches, keeping the knees straight, using your backpack, cooler, a log, or a rock as a prop (Fig. 2-1). If breathing difficulty exists or if head injury is suspected, elevate the head and shoulders but not the legs (Fig. 2-2). If the victim is unconscious, the side-lying position should be used (Fig. 2-3).

Fig. 2-1: Shock position

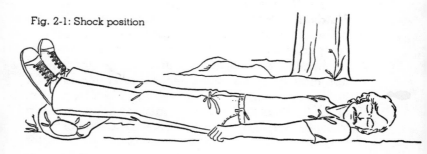

Fig. 2-2: Shock position when breathing is difficult or head is injured

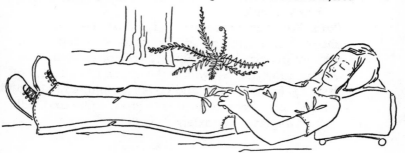

Fig. 2-3: Side-lying position for shock when victim is unconscious

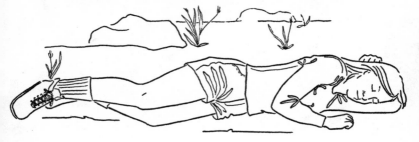

2. **Body Temperature:** The environmental temperature will determine the amount of covering needed. Extremes of either heat or cold are additional stresses and cannot be handled by the shock victim. Keep him covered just enough to avoid chilling. If it is cold or damp, blankets or sleeping bags should be placed underneath as well as over the victim to prevent heat loss to the ground. In warm environmental temperatures, a blanket to lie on may be all that is necessary.

3. **Fluids:** Fluids should be given only if medical care is delayed for an hour or more and there are no serious complications such as unconsciousness, semiconsciousness, or breathing difficulty. Moistening the lips may help the victim feel more comfortable. If fluids are given, water that contains 1 level teaspoon of salt (or 1 salt tablet) and ½ teaspoon of baking soda to each quart of water is suggested. The water should be neither cold nor hot, because extremes in water temperature could cause convulsions or vomiting. Do not give the victim alcoholic beverages, as they may induce vomiting.

4. **Pain:** Pain can cause and/or increase the degree of shock. Certain things can be done to reduce pain without giving drugs, which may not be available and usually are not within the scope of immediate first aid. Immobilizing and covering injuries help to relieve pain. Reassurance is of great value and will reduce the level of anxiety.

3

Choking, Respiratory and Circulatory Emergencies

CHOKING

Choking is one of the most common life-threatening emergencies and may be caused by food, small objects, vomitus, water, or anything that fits into the mouth. Signs of airway obstruction can easily be recognized. If the obstruction is partial the hand goes to the throat, there may be high-pitched noises while attempting to breath in air, and the face becomes blue. The coughing efforts are weak and ineffective. If the victim can breathe or cough at all, let him persist with his own efforts to expel the foreign object, but stay with him. If there is increasing breathing difficulty and he becomes unable to speak or cough, the airway is completely obstructed. The rescuer must proceed to relieve the obstruction and, if necessary, provide air to the victim. The purpose of the following techniques is to force air out from behind the foreign object, thereby dislodging and causing it to pop out.

Small child or infant: A small child or infant may be

Fig. 3-1: Administering back blows

turned upside down over the rescuer's arm and given sharp blows between the shoulder blades.

Adult: The victim may be either sitting, standing, or lying down.

Back Blows

1. Administer up to 4 sharp blows between the shoulder blades over the spine in rapid succession.
2. If the victim is lying down, turn him on his side and administer the back blows as above (Fig. 3-1).

If the back blows are ineffective, deliver up to 4 abdominal or chest thrusts in rapid succession.

Abdominal Thrusts

1. Stand behind the victim and wrap your arms around his waist.
2. Place the thumb side of your fist against the victim's abdomen, midway between the navel and the rib cage.
3. Grasp your fist with the other hand and press the victim's abdomen with a quick upward thrust. If necessary, repeat upward thrusts 4 times (Fig. 3-2).
4. If the victim is lying down, place on back, put both hands on upper abdomen, and follow the same procedure, pressing with heel of hands (Fig. 3-3).

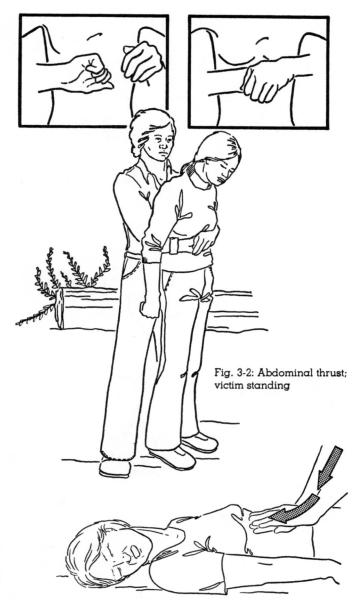

Fig. 3-2: Abdominal thrust;
victim standing

Fig. 3-3: Abdominal thrust; victim lying

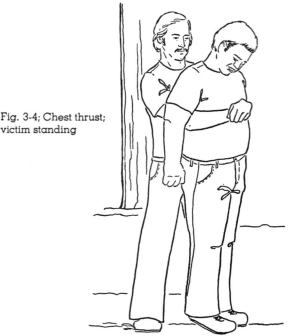

Fig. 3-4; Chest thrust; victim standing

Chest Thrusts

This technique is used when the victim is in advanced pregnancy or is obese and the rescuer cannot get his arms around the victim's waist.

If the victim is standing or sitting:

1. Stand behind the victim; place your arms under his armpits and around his chest (Fig. 3-4).
2. Place thumb side of your fist on the breastbone, above the xiphoid process (lower tip of the breastbone); see Fig. 3-17.
3. Grasp your fist and exert a quick backward thrust.

If the victim is lying down:

1. Kneel close to the side of the victim.
2. Place your hands on each side of the victim's chest, the heels of your hands at the level of the nipples and with your fingers curving around rib cage (Fig. 3-5).
3. With a squeezing motion, give a quick downward and inward thrust.
4. Repeat up to 4 times.

Repeat back blows and thrusts until they are effective or until unconsciousness occurs. If the victim becomes unconscious, use the following sequence.

1. Place victim on ground and prepare for artificial respiration.
2. Open airway by tilting head so chin is pointing upward (Fig. 3-7) by placing one hand on forehead and the other hand under the neck. If a neck or spinal injury is suspected, use a jaw thrust method by hooking your fingers on the angle of the jaw, and pulling forward (Fig. 3-8). Do not bend the neck, as further injuries could occur.
3. Attempt to manually remove the obstructing material (Fig. 3-6). When the victim is unconscious, it is easier to reach into the mouth with your index finger and hook the object.
4. Turn victim on side and give 4 back blows.
5. Turn victim on his back and give 4 thrusts.
6. Pinch nostrils (Fig. 3-9).
7. Attempt to breathe air into victim (Fig. 3-10).

Repeat steps 4 through 7. If this sequence does not work to relieve the obstruction in 4 repeats, then the victim will require artificial respiration to provide him with air until medical assistance is available.

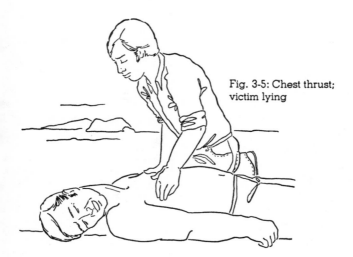

Fig. 3-5: Chest thrust; victim lying

MOUTH-TO-MOUTH ARTIFICIAL RESPIRATION

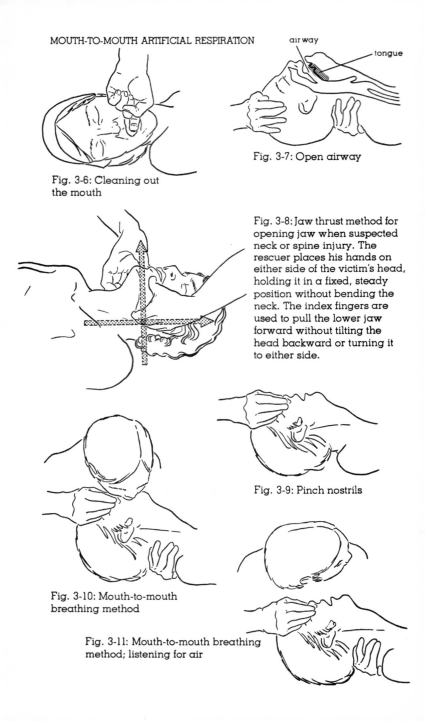

Fig. 3-6: Cleaning out the mouth

Fig. 3-7: Open airway

Fig. 3-8: Jaw thrust method for opening jaw when suspected neck or spine injury. The rescuer places his hands on either side of the victim's head, holding it in a fixed, steady position without bending the neck. The index fingers are used to pull the lower jaw forward without tilting the head backward or turning it to either side.

Fig. 3-9: Pinch nostrils

Fig. 3-10: Mouth-to-mouth breathing method

Fig. 3-11: Mouth-to-mouth breathing method; listening for air

RESPIRATORY EMERGENCIES

A respiratory emergency is one in which normal breathing stops or is reduced. This could be due to many causes, such as drowning, crushed chest, lightning, asthma, severe allergic reactions to insect bites, as well as choking. Permanent brain damage is very likely to result if a person is without oxygen for 4 – 6 minutes, and it is almost assured if oxygen lack is longer. As a rescuer in the outdoors, your job is to ventilate the lungs immediately and allow air to be exhaled by the victim. The best methods to use for lung ventilation are the mouth-to-mouth, the mouth-to-nose, or the mouth-to-mouth-and-nose methods.

Artificial Respiration

MOUTH-TO-MOUTH METHOD:
1. Place the victim on his back.
2. If any foreign matter is visible in the mouth such as food, vomitus, dentures, or gum, remove it quickly with your index finger, sweeping from side to side (Fig. 3-6).
3. Tilt the head so the chin is pointing upward (Fig. 3-7). If a neck or spinal injury is suspected, use a jaw thrust method by hooking your fingers on the angle of the jaw, and pulling forward (Fig. 3-8). Do not bend the neck, as further injuries could occur.
4. Pinch the nostrils. This will prevent air from escaping through the nose (Fig. 3-9).
5. Open your mouth wide and take a deep breath. Place your mouth over the victim's, making sure your mouth makes an airtight seal over the victim's mouth (Fig. 3-10). Then breathe into the victim at the rate of 12 times per minute or once every 5 seconds.
6. Watch the victim's chest. When you see the chest rise, stop blowing, remove your mouth, place your ear next to the victim's mouth, and listen for air leaving the lungs (Fig. 3-11).

Fig. 3-12: Removing air from the stomach

7. If you are not getting air exchange with the victim, reposition his head (Fig. 3-7). The victim's tongue could be blocking the air passage thereby making air exchange impossible.
8. Once air has been exhaled, repeat the blowing-listening cycle until the victim is breathing normally.
9. If the victim's stomach is bulging, air may have been blown into it. Inflation of the stomach is not danger-ous, although it may make lung ventilation more difficult and may increase the likelihood of vomiting. If the stomach is bulging, turn the victim's head to one side, then press your hand briefly but firmly over the upper abdomen between the rib margin and the navel (Fig. 3-12). Make sure to clean out the mouth if any visible matter appears.

Fig. 3-13 and 3-14: Mouth-to-nose breathing method

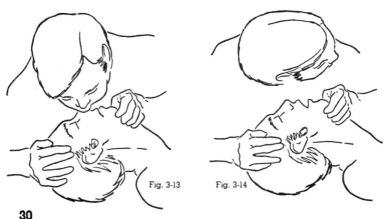

Fig. 3-13   Fig. 3-14

MOUTH-TO-NOSE METHOD: If a person is suffering from a broken jaw or is experiencing severe bleeding in the mouth, then the mouth-to-nose method should be used. Position the victim as for the mouth-to-mouth method and clear the mouth as before, but breathe into the victim's nose and close his mouth (Fig. 3-13). Rate of breathing is the same as for mouth-to-mouth method. On the exhalation phase, open the victim's mouth to allow the air to escape (Fig. 3-14).

MOUTH-TO-MOUTH-AND-NOSE METHOD FOR IN-FANTS AND SMALL CHILDREN: When giving artificial respiration to an infant or small child, the rescuer covers both the mouth and nose with his mouth, blows with the breath in his cheeks at a rate of 20 to 30 times a minute or once every 2 – 3 seconds (Fig. 3-15). Allow air to escape on exhalation phase.

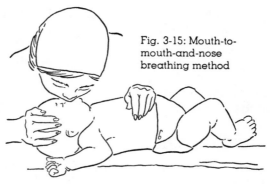

Fig. 3-15: Mouth-to-mouth-and-nose breathing method

CIRCULATORY EMERGENCIES

When a person stops breathing, we supply air to their lungs with artificial respiration. When his heart stops beating and the body is no longer circulating blood, we can do the heart's work by externally massaging the heart to provide an artificial circulation. The combination of artificial respiration and artificial circulation is called Cardiopulmonary Resuscitation or CPR. A life may be saved with the

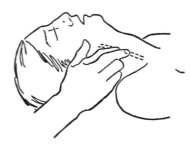

Fig. 3-16: Feeling the neck
(carotid) pulse

early recognition of a stopped heart and the proper use of CPR techniques. A stopped heart is recognized by the absence of a pulse in the large artery in the neck near the angle of the jaw (Fig. 3-16) and by the absence of breathing.

> **CPR is to be immediately initiated only when it can be determined that _both_ breathing and heartbeat have stopped, since the compression might interfere with the heart's normal functioning.**

We strongly recommend that all members of your camping, hiking, or backpacking group be skilled in CPR. Check with the local American Red Cross, American Heart Association or community college for free course offerings in your area.

The ABCs of CPR

ABC stands for airway, breathing, and circulation. If the pulse is absent, breathing is absent, and the victim has a deathlike appearance, effective circulation has ceased, and CPR must be started immediately. The victim must be on a firm surface with the rescuer kneeling by the side of the victim.

ONE-RESCUER CPR FOR ADULTS:
Airway
1. Clean out the mouth (Fig. 3-6).
2. Tilt head by placing one hand on the forehead and the other under the neck. This prevents the tongue from falling back to obstruct the airway (Fig. 3-7).

Breathing

1. With the airway open, check for breathing with your ear over the nose and mouth of the victim and your eyes watching the chest (Fig. 3-11). If victim is not breathing, start breathing for him as follows:

2. Cover the victim's mouth with yours while pinching the nostrils with the fingers of the hand on the forehead (Fig. 3-9 and 3-10).

3. Give 4 initial quick lung inflations without allowing time for full exhalation by the victim. This will give him a temporary supply of air.

Circulation

1. Check pulse in neck for 5 – 10 seconds (Fig. 3-16). If there is no pulse, start chest compression as follows:

2. Measure 2 fingers width up from the lower tip (xiphoid process) of the breastbone (sternum) (Fig. 3-17).

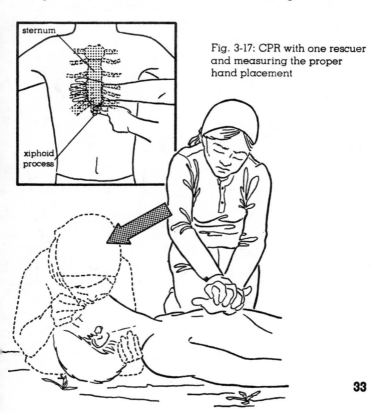

Fig. 3-17: CPR with one rescuer and measuring the proper hand placement

33

3. Place the heel of one hand at this point of the breastbone, with other hand on top of the first one, and start compression. Compressions should be smooth, with downward pressure being applied while keeping the elbows straight. Compress the breastbone of the adult 1½ − 2 inches, at the rate of once a second. Release pressure between compressions, but do not remove hands from the breastbone.
4. Compress 15 times, then give 2 breaths without allowing time for exhalation (Fig. 3-17).
5. Continue the cycle in this manner with 15 compressions, then 2 breaths. This will supply approximately 80 compressions and 12 lung inflations per minute.
6. Check the pulse periodically to see if CPR has been effective (Fig. 3-16).

CPR is continued until breathing and heart beat start again, you are too exhausted to continue, medical or paramedical help arrive, or the victim is pronounced dead by medical personnel.

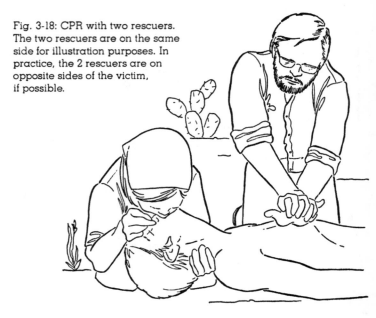

Fig. 3-18: CPR with two rescuers. The two rescuers are on the same side for illustration purposes. In practice, the 2 rescuers are on opposite sides of the victim, if possible.

TWO-RESCUER CPR FOR ADULTS:

1. One rescuer is at the victim's side and performs the external heart compressions without interruption while the other rescuer is at the head, keeping airway open and continuing artificial respiration (Fig. 3-18).
2. The uninterrupted compressions are counted out loud at the rate of once a second and the rescuer at the head quickly breathes in the victim at the count of 5, a ratio of 1 lung inflation for every 5 compressions.

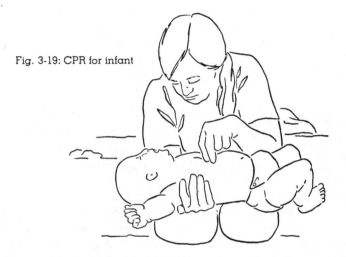

Fig. 3-19: CPR for infant

CPR MODIFICATIONS FOR INFANTS AND CHILDREN:

1. For infants, depress the *middle* of the breastbone approximately ½ inch at the rate of 100 – 120 compressions per minute, using only 2 fingers (Fig. 3-19).
2. For children, depress the breastbone about 1 inch at the rate of 80 – 100 times per minute, using only the heel of one hand.
3. In breathing for the infant or small child, the rescuer covers both the mouth and nose of the infant with his mouth, and blows puffs of air from his cheeks at the rate of 30 times a minute or once every 2 seconds (Fig. 3-15). The rate for a child is 20 times a minute or once every 3 seconds.

4

Poisoning

A poison is any substance that, when ingested, inhaled, absorbed, applied to the skin, or developed within the body, in relatively small amounts, produces injury to the body by its chemical action. The backpacker, camper, or fisherman has the potential for exposure to a wide variety of toxic substances. Whether or not the substance is toxic to an individual will depend upon the quantity of the substance, the amount of exposure to the substance, and the age and size of the individual. The treatment of acute poisoning is always an emergency, and proper first aid may save a life. The aim of first-aid measures is to help prevent absorption of the poison, therefore *speed* is essential. Initial treatment will consist of removal of the poison, the delay of its absorption, an antidote if available, and supportive measures, such as artificial respiration.

INGESTED POISONS
FOOD AND WATER POISONING

Poisoning from food and water is a sudden, explosive illness that occurs after ingestion of food or drink that contains a poisonous or irritating substance. The sources are: contaminated, inadequately refrigerated, or improperly cooked foods, contaminated water, wild plants, wild berries, poisonous mushrooms (Fig. 4-1), shellfish (mussels, clams, oysters, abalone), or eels.

SYMPTOMS: The symptoms and time of their onset will vary depending upon the source. Foods that are contaminated, inadequately refrigerated, or improperly cooked may cause the following symptoms:

- *Botulism* poisoning symptoms develop within 18 – 24 hours after ingestion and could include fatigue, generalized muscle weakness, dizziness, headache, vision disturbances, difficulty in swallowing and in speech, respiratory failure, and coma. Diarrhea does not usually occur.
- *Bacterial* poisoning symptoms develop within 2 – 6 hours, and weakness, dizziness, nausea and vomiting, severe abdominal cramping, severe diarrhea, and elevated temperature may occur.

WILD POISONOUS PLANTS, MUSHROOMS, OR BERRIES will cause the following symptoms in 6 hours or more after eating: sudden severe abdominal pain, nausea and vomiting, bloody diarrhea, extreme thirst, dehydration, excessive tearing and salivation, weakness, hallucinations, confusion, excitability, bluish skin color, respiratory failure, and heart failure if untreated. Unless you are an expert, forget about eating any mushrooms. If you think you are an expert and you are sure a fungus is an edible

white gills

ring

Fig. 4-1: Poisonous Mushroom

"Death's Cup" bulbous base

one, taste a tiny scraping from the fungus; poisonous mushrooms often taste poisonous.

SHELLFISH such as mussels, clams, oysters, and abalone are potentially poisonous if eaten during the months of June through October. The symptoms will begin within half an hour and include nausea and vomiting, severe abdominal cramping, muscle weakness and paralysis of the extremities, and respiratory failure. Diarrhea does not usually occur.

EELS AND SOME FISH in different areas of the world are poisonous and may not be eaten any time of the year. If you plan to take a fishing trip in unknown or unfamiliar country, check out the edible and unedible ones with the fish-and-game authorities. The symptoms of poisoning may start up to 36 hours after eating. They are varied and may include tingling of the lips, gums, tongue, and face, hives, severe itching of the skin, blotchy skin rash, vomiting, abdominal pain, joint and muscle pain, paralysis, respiratory failure, headache, swelling of the tongue, and difficulty in breathing due to the swelling of the vocal cords.

CONTAMINATED WATER may cause nausea and vomiting, abdominal cramping, and diarrhea, but it will be less severe than food poisoning.

TREATMENT: While you are starting the treatment, answer the following questions:

- How long after eating did the symptoms occur? If immediately after, this suggests shellfish poisoning. If the symptoms occur some time after eating, 2 hours or more, this suggests contaminated foods, wild poisonous plants, or eels and fish.
- What was eaten or drunk in the previous meal? Was there an unusual smell or taste? Most foods that cause bacterial poisoning do not have a bad smell or taste.
- Is there vomiting? What does the vomit look like? You may be able to identify the substance from the undigested particles.

- Is there diarrhea? This is usually absent with botulism, shellfish, or other fish poisoning.
- Does the victim have any symptoms that indicate nervous system involvement? This is seen in botulism poisoning.
- Is there fever? This is present in some bacterial and fish poisoning.

1. Induce vomiting to empty the stomach by tickling the back of the throat.

   Do not induce vomiting if the victim is unconscious, convulsing, or if the poison is a strong acid, alkali (such as lye or bleach), or petroleum product (such as butane or gasoline).

2. Have the victim lie down. Refer to Figure 2-3 for position if victim is vomiting.
3. Maintain body temperature. See Chapter 2, "Shock."
4. Control nausea with sips of weak tea or carbonated drinks, if available.
5. Treat diarrhea, if it continues, with antidiarrheal drugs such as Lomotil (no more than 3 pills in 24 hours unless otherwise directed by your doctor) or Kaopectate, and apply warm compresses to the abdomen to relieve spasms.
6. Replace fluids about 12 – 24 hours after nausea and vomiting subside.
7. Artificial respiration may be necessary in instances of botulism or fish poisoning.
8. Transport victim to a medical facility for emergency treatment of botulism, fish, and mushroom poisoning.

INHALED POISONS

Gases and smoke from the combustion of certain fuels act as poisons by depriving the respiratory and circulatory systems of available oxygen. All wood and charcoal fires as well as camping heaters should be burned in well-ventilated areas and never in enclosed tents, campers, or vans.

SYMPTOMS: The symptoms are headache, lethargy, drowsiness, coma, and convulsions. If the poison is carbon monoxide, the skin will sometimes be cherry-red in color.

TREATMENT:

1. *Carry* victim to fresh air immediately. (Walking will use up too much oxygen.)
2. Loosen all tight clothing.
3. Maintain body temperature. Prevent chilling.
4. Keep victim as quiet as possible. Avoid jarring or noise.
5. Do not give alcohol in *any* form.
6. Give artificial respiration if breathing stops.
7. Medical assistance is necessary if condition progresses to coma and convulsion.

CONTACT POISONS

Poison ivy (Fig. 4-2), poison oak (Fig. 4-3), and poison sumac (Fig. 4-4) are common sources of contact poisoning for the person who gets away from the well-frequented trails.

Susceptible skin reacts to contact with the oils of these plants. This oil, urushiol, is present in all parts of the plant, including dead stems and roots. Contact with the plants need not be direct. Indirect contact with the oil may come from handling contaminated clothing, tools, or animals or from inhaling the smoke of burning plants. The smoke contains oil droplets and could cause serious inflammation of the nose, throat, and lungs.

Contact poisoning from these plants can't always be prevented, but may be minimized by recognizing and avoiding the major offenders, by wearing protective clothing in highly infested areas, by removing the contaminated clothing as soon as possible, and by washing yourself immediately.

Fig. 4-2: Poison Ivy; Eastern Coast

Size: Small plant in forest; vine or shrub in more open areas; glossy, smooth-edged leaflets in groups of 3; small berries

Color: Clusters of small, greenish-white to cream flowers that bloom after leaves appear in the spring; Fruit is greenish when young and tan to yellow when ripe; leaves are red in autumn

Habitat: East of the Rockies and Cascades; on flood plains, bottom lands, lake shores, and sand dunes; also found in Mexico

Fig. 4-3: Western Poison Oak

Size: Vine or shrub; oaklike leaflets in groups of 3; small berries

Color: Flowers and fruit similar to poison ivy; leaves turn red in the autumn

Habitat: Western North America from southern British Columbia to northern Baja; from the Pacific Coast to the Cascade and Sierra mountains

Fig. 4-4: Poison Sumac

Size: Tall shrub up to 15 feet in height; leaves with 7 to 11 smooth-edged bright green leaflets; small berries

Color: Abundant small, greenish white to cream flowers; glossy, pale yellow or cream fruits, nonpoisonous sumac has red fruit

Habitat: Predominately found east of the Mississippi in bogs, swamps, wet bottom land, while the nonpoisonous sumac is never found in wet places.

41

SYMPTOMS: Skin eruptions may develop in hours or even days after contact. The skin will burn and itch, feel bumpy, and eventually form blisters. In the more severe cases, where there are large blistered areas, swelling may occur. If the oils have been inhaled, the symptoms will include swelling of the tissues in the nose, throat, and lungs. Respiratory difficulties may develop; they will require immediate professional medical care.

TREATMENT:

1. Carefully remove all contaminated clothing for washing.
2. Wash skin with soap and hot water and rinse well.
3. Do not scratch. This can lead to a secondary infection.
4. Apply a soothing lotion such as a calamine or a cortisone cream like Synalar to the affected areas. Apply thinly and avoid covering too much of the body's surface with any ointment or lotion. Be extremely careful applying anything around the eyes.
5. If blistering and oozing develop, use cold, wet compresses of saline solution (six salt tablets or 2 tablespoons of salt in a pint of water).
6. Antihistamines can relieve itching but must be used carefully. Side effects include drowsiness and a reduced ability to make quick decisions.

ABSORBED POISONS

Poisoning by Snakebite

There are four major kinds of poisonous snakes in the United States. They are the rattlesnake (Fig. 4-5), water moccasin or "cottonmouth" (Fig. 4-6), copperhead (Fig. 4-7), and coral snake (Fig. 4-8).

The first three are *pit vipers*, so called because of a small pit between the nostril and eye on each side of the head. The bite of the pit viper leaves a very distinctive mark, which is distinguishable from the bite of a nonpoisonous snake (Fig. 4-9). Always examine the bite before begin-

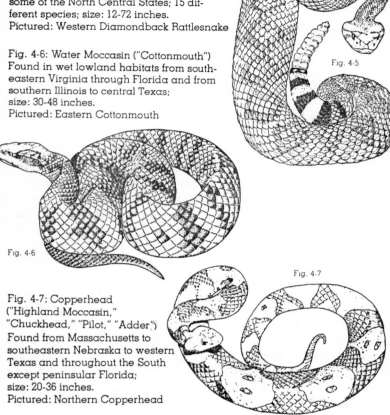

Fig. 4-5: Rattlesnake
Found throughout North America except in some of the North Central States; 15 different species; size: 12-72 inches.
Pictured: Western Diamondback Rattlesnake

Fig. 4-6: Water Moccasin ("Cottonmouth")
Found in wet lowland habitats from southeastern Virginia through Florida and from southern Illinois to central Texas; size: 30-48 inches.
Pictured: Eastern Cottonmouth

Fig. 4-5

Fig. 4-6

Fig. 4-7: Copperhead
("Highland Moccasin,"
"Chuckhead," "Pilot," "Adder")
Found from Massachusetts to southeastern Nebraska to western Texas and throughout the South except peninsular Florida; size: 20-36 inches.
Pictured: Northern Copperhead

Fig. 4-7

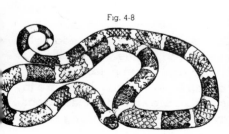

Fig. 4-8

Fig. 4-8: Coral Snake
("Candy-stick Snake")
Found from Southeastern North Carolina to Florida, and west through southern Arkansas to west-central Texas; also found in central Arizona and southwestern New Mexico; size: 15-30 inches.
Pictured: Eastern Coral Snake

43

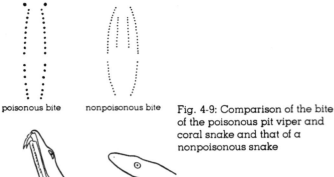

poisonous bite   nonpoisonous bite

Fig. 4-9: Comparison of the bite of the poisonous pit viper and coral snake and that of a nonpoisonous snake

ning immediate first-aid measures. A person bitten by a nonpoisonous variety of snake need not be subjected to the first-aid actions necessary in the case of a bite by a poisonous snake. The bite of the pit viper comes as a lightninglike strike, injecting a small amount of venom from two fangs in the forward portion of the upper jaw, which leave two distinctive puncture wounds at the point of entry. The bite of the nonpoisonous variety differs from the poisonous ones in that there are six rows of teeth marks—four rows from the teeth of the upper jaw and two from the teeth of the lower jaw (Fig. 4-9). If someone is bitten by a nonpoisonous snake, treat the bite as you would for any puncture wound.

The small *coral snake*, which is marked with bands of red and black and narrow bands of yellow, bites in an extremely different manner. Coral snakes, which are very dangerous, strike humans relatively rarely, but when they do, they bite and hang on, sinking their fangs beneath the skin and chew for as long as a minute. The snake will release after the bite. The bite mark is similar to that of the pit viper, except not as distinct. The venom is exceedingly toxic and acts as a nerve poison, while the pit viper's venom acts mainly as a blood and tissue poison.

Most snakebites occur on the legs or hands. If you are in an area where poisonous snakes are known to exist, wear suitable attire. It is strongly recommended that long pants, boots, and gloves be worn in this type of country.

44

SYMPTOMS: The symptoms vary greatly and depend upon the size of the victim, the amount of venom injected, the speed of absorption, and the location of the bite. Generally, a bite by a *pit viper* will cause severe pain, characterized by rapid swelling and discoloration of the skin at the bite area. Other conditions may develop such as general body weakness, rapid pulse, nausea and vomiting, shortness of breath, dimness of vision, shock, and, occasionally, death. The *coral snake* bite will be characterized by only slight burning pain and mild local swelling at the wound site, blurred vision, drooping eyelids, drowsiness, increased saliva and sweating, sometimes nausea and vomiting, respiratory difficulty, paralysis, shock, convulsions, coma, and possible death.

TREATMENT: In recent years, the incidence of snakebite in this country has increased, because more and more people are involved in outdoor recreational activities. All backpackers and campers should know the treatment for snakebite and be able to initiate it quickly and calmly. No single treatment devised so far is completely successful; in some instances, death still occurs. The most important and immediate measure is to keep the victim quiet, and to reassure him. Once he is quiet, begin immediate emergency treatment.

Primary Treatment

1. Immobilize the bitten arm or leg so that the bite is below the level of the victim's heart.
2. If the bite is on an arm or leg, apply a constricting band 2 – 4 inches above the bite, not on a joint, between the wound and the victim's heart (Fig. 4-10).

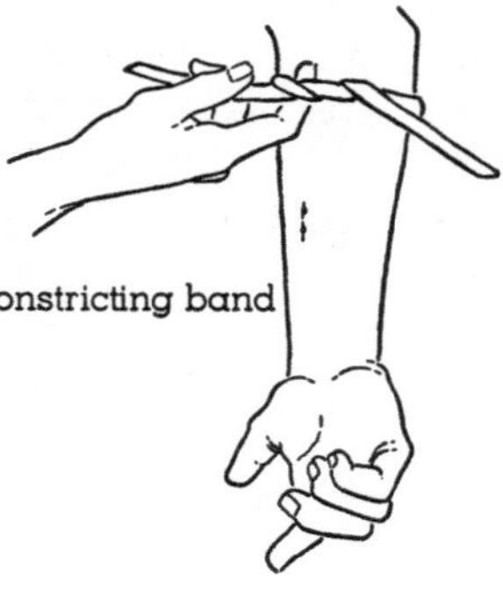

Fig. 4-10: Applying a constricting band

The constricting band should not be tight; if properly applied there will be some oozing from the wound. You should be able to slip your index finger under the band. Remember this is *not* a tourniquet application. The purpose of the constricting band is to stop the capillary action, not to restrict deep blood flow in the arteries and veins.

3. Use the blade that comes in a snakebite kit, if available; otherwise sterilize a knifeblade with a flame and make an incision through the skin approximately ⅛ – ¼ inch deep and no longer than ½ inch at the points of suspected venom deposit. Be extremely careful to make incisions through the skin only and lengthwise on the limb (Fig. 4-10). Do not make a crosscut incision. Special care should always be taken when making incisions not to cut so deeply that further disability is caused from severed nerves, muscles, and tendons; cutting lengthwise reduces this risk.

4. Apply suction with the suction cup contained in the snakebite kit, if available; otherwise use your mouth. Snake venom is not a stomach poison, but mouth suction should *not* be used if a rescuer has any open sores in the mouth. Suction should be continued for at least 60 minutes. If swelling extends up to the original constricting band, apply another a few inches above the first. leaving the first one in place.

5. A cold, wet cloth or ice wrapped in a cloth could be used over the wound to help slow down the absorption of the poison.

Secondary Treatment

1. Wash the wounds thoroughly with soap and water. Apply a sterile dressing and bandage it in place.

2. Do not give alcohol in any form. Alcohol dilates the blood vessels of the skin and increases absorption of the poison.

3. Treat for shock.

4. Give artificial respiration, if necessary.

5. Move victim slowly, preferably by stretcher or cot.
6. Consult a physician with regard to antivenin therapy.

Poisoning by Marine Life

Many marine animals can produce puncture wounds and inject poisons that will have varying effects on individuals, depending upon their sensitivity or resistance and the amount of venom injected.

JELLYFISH AND PORTUGUESE MAN-OF-WAR: The jellyfish (Fig. 4-11) and Portuguese man-of-war (Fig. 4-12) have stinging cells located on tentacles that discharge venom through threadlike tubes upon contact. The venom produces a rash with minute hemorrhages in the skin, muscular cramping, nausea and vomiting, shock, and sometimes respiratory failure.

TREATMENT:
1. Wipe off the affected area with a towel and wash with a diluted solution of ammonia and water followed by hot Epsom or table salt soaks (2 tablespoons in a pint of water). The soaks will relieve the pain.
2. It has been suggested that the toxin may be deactivated by applying an organic solvent such as mineral spirits, kerosene, or gasoline. Such treatment is not effective unless applied promptly, as the toxin may quickly enter the bloodstream.

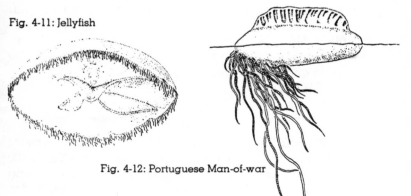

Fig. 4-11: Jellyfish

Fig. 4-12: Portuguese Man-of-war

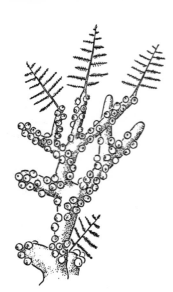

Fig. 4-14: Cone Shell

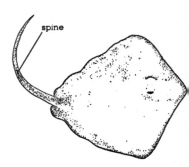

Fig. 4-13: Stinging Coral

Fig. 4-15: Stingray

STINGING CORAL: One variety of coral is the stinging or fire coral (Fig. 4-13). It is common in waters around Florida, the West Indies, and the Caribbean. It is not easily distinguishable from other coral. The points of the coral contain stinging cells, which, when touched, penetrate the skin and release venom. If you plan to swim in the area of coral, wear canvas shoes and possibly a scuba wet suit. If you are shell and coral collecting, wear heavy gloves.

SYMPTOMS: The symptoms include intense local burning sensation, bleeding, pain, and a rash around the multiple cuts on the skin.

TREATMENT:

1. Treat as a wound (see Chapter 1).
2. If there is a severe reaction, seek medical help.

CONE SHELL: The cone shell (Fig. 4-14) is a type of mollusk related to the snail. There are between 400 and 500 different species, of various colors, and in sizes ranging from 8 to 60 inches in length. They are generally located in shallow water in tropical seas and are usually associated with the coral reefs. When handled, they eject a venomous dart from the open end, penetrating the victim.

SYMPTOMS: Initially there is a burning sting at the point where the dart has entered the skin; numbness follows accompanied by a tingling sensation spreading over the body, most noticeable in the mouth and on the lips. Paralysis and heart failure will follow if not treated.

TREATMENT:

1. Apply a constricting band (Fig. 4-10).
2. Soak affected area in hot water for 30 minutes or use hot compresses.
3. If symptoms become severe, CPR may be necessary until medical help arrives (see Chapter 3).

STINGRAY: Stingrays (Fig. 4-15) are found around the world in temperate and tropical seas. More people are injured by stingrays than all other fish combined. They cruise along sandy bottoms, partially bury themselves in mud or sand when resting, and are virtually invisible even in clear water with a coloring that blends into the surrounding. A poison is contained in the one or more spines located on top of the tail. If stepped on or bumped, the stingray will whip up its tail in an attempt to get away. The spine of the tail tears or penetrates the skin and frequently becomes imbedded. If possible, the spine should be removed immediately.

If the spine is imbedded deeply, it is best to let medical personnel remove it, since removal will severely tear the deeper tissues.

SYMPTOMS: Symptoms include acute pain at the time of injury, bleeding from the puncture wound, abdominal and muscle cramps, and shock.

TREATMENT:

1. Irrigate the wound immediately with the salt water at hand; this will help wash out the poison.
2. Apply a constricting band (Fig. 4-10).
3. Soak the wound in *hot* water for 30 to 90 minutes. The water should be as hot as can be tolerated. This will help to further destroy the toxin.

4. Remove any loose fragments of the spine that can be seen.
5. Obtain medical help for further treatment and tetanus protection.

PREVENTION: Swimmers should slide their feet along the bottom of the water, rather than taking steps. The sliding will warn the stingray and it will move out of the way.

SALTWATER CATFISH: The saltwater catfish (Fig. 4-16) is widely distributed in the oceans, and can be 2 feet or more in length. It has a venomous, saw-toothed spine at the base of the large dorsal fin. This spine tears the skin and introduces venom into the victim. The fish itself is not poisonous to eat.

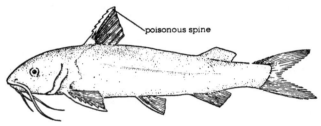
poisonous spine

Fig. 4-16: Saltwater Catfish

SYMPTOMS: The symptoms include pain, swelling, bleeding, abdominal and muscle cramps, and shock.
TREATMENT: Treat as you would a stingray wound.
PREVENTION: Learn to handle the catfish properly when it is hooked and landed. Protect your hands with gloves or a heavy cloth and be aware of the location of the spine.

Poisoning by Insects

HORNETS, WASPS, ANTS, YELLOW JACKETS, BEES: These insects (Fig. 4-17) are widely distributed throughout the world. They sting when disturbed or annoyed. Burning, itching with localized swelling, and red-

Fig. 4-17

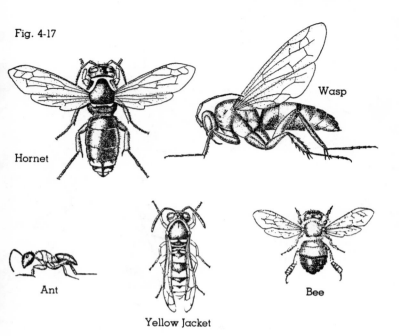

Hornet

Wasp

Ant

Yellow Jacket

Bee

ness occur. Occasionally a more serious reaction will occur due to multiple bites or due to an acute allergic response to the venom.

SYMPTOMS: Symptoms include hives, swelling of the throat with breathing difficulties, headache, nausea, shock, and unconsciousness (see "Allergic Reactions" in Chapter 7).

TREATMENT:

1. If the reaction is mild, remove the stinger immediately by scraping if off gently with a sharp object, like a knife. Do not squeeze the stinger since this will force the remaining venom into the tissues.

2. Wash well with soap and water.

3. Apply cold compresses for 30 minutes.

4. If the victim is known to be sensitive to bee stings, he should be carrying a special emergency kit with specific drugs. Administer according to instructions. If he does not have an emergency kit and he is known to be sensitive to bee stings or is suffering from a severe

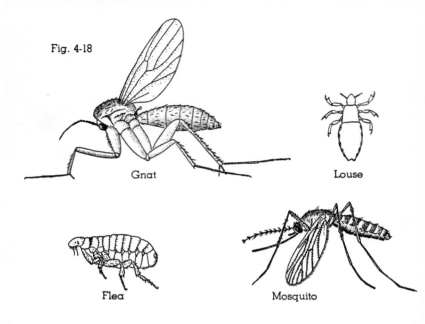

Fig. 4-18

Gnat

Louse

Flea

Mosquito

reaction, remove stinger if possible, administer an antihistamine, apply cool sponges, and transport to a medical facility.

GNATS, LICE, FLEAS, MOSQUITOES: (Fig. 4-18) Bites from these insects cause a local pain and irritation but are not likely to lead to any more than that.

TREATMENT: Treat the same as for hornets, wasps, bees, yellow jackets, and ants.

TICKS: Ticks (Fig. 4-19) are oval shaped with a dark head, are gray or brown in color, and measure ⅛ – ¼ inch when mature. They are parasitic animals related to spi-

Fig. 4-19: Tick

ders and scorpions. They are found throughout the United States. Ticks often trouble people who are walking and camping in the woods. They bury their head under the victim's skin, drawing blood in through a beak. This beak has strong teeth, which are bent backward, helping the parasite to cling tightly to the victim. The tick must be totally removed since it can transmit such diseases as Rocky Mountain Spotted Fever. There is also a danger of infection if any of the mouthparts are left in the wound.

TREATMENT:

1. Do not pull the tick off, as the head will stay in.
2. Cover the tick with any available heavy oil such as salad, machine, or mineral oil, or use Vaseline or Chapstick. This should disengage the tick at once, but if it does not, leave the oil in place for 30 minutes.
3. Remove the tick gently with tweezers.
4. Wash well with soap and water.

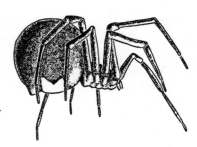

Fig. 4-20: Black Widow Spider

BLACK WIDOW SPIDERS: A bite by a black widow spider (Fig. 4-20) is generally quite serious, but is not necessarily fatal. The black widow spider is about ¾ – 1½ inches long and is easily identified by the hourglass-shaped red spot on its belly.

SYMPTOMS: The black widow spider can cause serious abdominal pain due to muscle spasm. Other symptoms include dilated pupils, generalized swelling of the face and extremities, and, occasionally, difficulties in breathing and speaking.

Fig. 4-21: Brown Recluse Spider

TREATMENT:
1. Cleanse the bite area thoroughly and wash with hydrogen peroxide, alcohol, or other antiseptic.
2. Cold compresses and soothing lotions such as a calamine can also be used.

BROWN RECLUSE SPIDER: The brown recluse spider (Fig. 4-21) is brownish in color and has a somewhat flattened body that averages ½ – ⅝ inch long, and has a dark-brown marking, shaped somewhat like an hourglass or violin, on its underside.

SYMPTOMS: Symptoms vary from severe local reactions to chills, fever, pains in the joints, and a localized rash around the bite area.

TREATMENT:
1. Follow the treatment for bites of black widow spiders.
2. If you have any type of antihistamine, you may give it.
3. Treat for shock.
4. Get medical help as soon as possible.

TARANTULA: Bites of tarantulas (Fig. 4-22) have similar

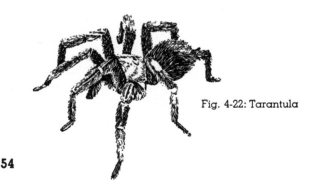

Fig. 4-22: Tarantula

effects as those of the black widow spider. Tarantulas are easily identified as rather large, hairy spiders, dark brown to black in color, 6 – 7 inches in length, and are commonly found in bananas and fruit shipped from other countries and in dry foothill areas.

TREATMENT:
1. Wash area with soap and water.
2. Apply cold compresses to the bite area.
3. Relieve pain with aspirin.
4. Seek medical help if bite becomes infected.

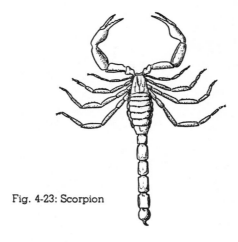

Fig. 4-23: Scorpion

SCORPION: The scorpion (Fig. 4-23) is a nocturnal land animal. Stings of scorpions are usually not considered serious. The scorpion ranges in size from ¾ inch to over 8 inches in length and is solid yellow or yellow with black stripes on the back. It is found in tropical areas and deserts, with the lethal types found in Arizona. It will hide in shoes, boots, and sleeping bags. It has a single, curved stinger in the tip of the tail. When alarmed, the scorpion will arch its tail up over the rest of the body. The stinger is then ready to jab forward, strike, and inject venom.

SYMPTOMS: There is a burning, tingling sensation at the site of the bite, followed by severe pain and swelling.

Muscle cramps, nausea and vomiting, headache, dizziness, excessive perspiration, high temperature, drooling, breathing difficulty, and occasionally convulsions and shock may develop.

TREATMENT:

1. Apply a constricting band (Fig. 4-10).
2. Keep the victim quiet.
3. Wash area with soap and water.
4. Apply ice packs or cold compresses.
5. If the reaction is severe, seek medical help for antivenin.

5

Bone and Muscle
Injuries

Injuries to the skeletal system include sprains, strains, dislocations, and fractures. The injuries can range all the way from very mild, with a minimum of interference in your camping or hiking activities, to very serious ones requiring medical assistance, as in a spinal fracture. Immediate, skillful first aid can mean the difference between full recovery or further injury, shock and deformity.

Accidents can't always be prevented, but certain precautions may be taken. Since falls account for almost all types of fractures, sprains, and the like, the hiker should have tightly laced, well-fitting boots with special soles that minimize slipping. He shouldn't hike while fatigued or when he feels he must hurry, as errors in judgment about distances, terrain, or footing result.

A few general principles of first aid for injuries to the skeletal structure must be followed. They are:

- Keep victim flat on his back at rest as long as he is unconscious or until you can determine what the injuries may be. Look first for evidence of injuries to the head, chest, or spine.
- If the victim must be transported while unconscious,

keep him flat on his back with head slightly elevated until he is sufficiently conscious to point out areas of pain or tenderness.

- If a back injury is suspected, take every precaution to avoid motion of the spine. The spinal cord may be damaged by fragments of bone rubbing against it if the spine is moved.
- If an arm or leg is broken, make it as immobile as possible before transporting the victim.
- If possible, elevate the immobilized extremity while transporting, to reduce swelling and pain.
- Do not try to set or line up broken bones. Splinting will be a temporary measure to reduce pain and shock by preventing the broken ends and adjacent joints from moving during transportation. After fractures have been splinted, make sure circulation is maintained in the injured part by checking for the pulse every half hour. If no pulse is felt, you may have to loosen the splint or take it off.
- Shock should be anticipated, even if the injury is not severe. Since it can be caused by fear as well as pain and hemorrhage, the rescuer's calm, knowledgeable, and reassuring manner will contribute to the prevention of shock. You should try to keep the victim as quiet and calm as possible, protect him from extremes in temperature, and have him lie down. The rescuer can also minimize shock by administering the appropriate first aid before obvious signs of shock appear.

FRACTURES

A fracture is a break in a bone. The break may be completely or incompletely through the bone, but the immediate first-aid treatment is the same. Most fractures happen when there is no control over the amount of force applied to the bone and/or when you are not prepared to resist or avoid the force. The type of force may be a direct blow, an indirect blow with the force transmitted to the site of the fracture, a penetrating injury, or a severe stress on the ligaments and muscles supporting a joint.

Fractures are classified as closed (simple) or open (compound). When the fractured surfaces are protected from contamination with the outside air by the overlying skin, the fracture is *closed*. If a wound occurs at the time of the fracture, so that air and therefore bacteria may be admitted, the fracture is *open*. An open fracture is more of a problem than a closed one, because the wound and the possibility of infection of the bone must be considered as well as the fracture. Injury to surrounding tissue by the fractured bone may be more of an emergency than the fracture itself. Nerves, blood vessels, ligaments, joints, lungs, the bladder, and other organs may be injured at the same time. Open fractures are to be treated as follows:

1. Control any serious bleeding by applying direct pressure (Fig. 1-1 through 1-3).

2. If there is bone protruding or if the pressure causes excessive pain, use pressure points (Fig. 1-4 through 1-10) to slow or stop the bleeding.

3. Cover the wound with a sterile dressing, bandage in place, and *then* immobilize the broken bone.

Immobilization is basic in first-aid treatment for fractures. In order to prevent further injury to soft tissues, keep

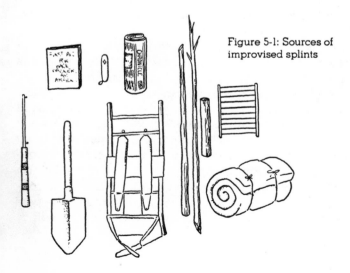

Figure 5-1: Sources of improvised splints

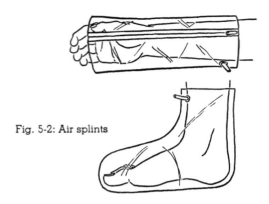

Fig. 5-2: Air splints

the fracture from moving by means of splints that extend above and below the fracture and by slings that decrease movement in the adjacent joints. Pieces of clothing may be used to secure improvised splints. Splints may be made from knives, tree limbs, fishing-pole handles, parts of your backpacking frame, cooking grates, shovels, tightly rolled sleeping bags, newspapers, or even this first-aid book (Fig. 5-1). You may wish to include commercial inflatable splints (Fig. 5-2) in your first-aid equipment if you plan to go deep into the wilderness areas.

FRACTURE OF THE HEAD, NECK, OR SPINE: Injuries to the head, neck, and spine can be serious and require close observation and careful first-aid treatment. If the victim has had a blow to the head or has hit it during a fall, treat for possible head injury (see Chapter 7, "Common Emergencies," "Head Injury"). If there are other symptoms such as blood or watery fluid coming from the ears, mouth, or nose, if the pupils of the eyes are unequal, or if there is a depression in the skull, treat as if the injury is a skull fracture. The treatment of a person with a possible skull fracture requires careful handling at all times to prevent further injury. The most important first step, if he is unconscious, is to maintain an open airway by placing him on his side with his head only slightly elevated. If he is conscious, he should remain absolutely quiet and not be permitted to get up and move around. If there is bleeding, apply a dressing lightly in place, without applying pressure, to avoid pushing bone fragments into the brain. Treat for shock (Chapter 2), immobilize (Fig. 5-3), and transport to a medical facility as soon as possible.

If there are neck and/or back injuries, always treat as if the spine is fractured. Unless there are hazards near the victim, such as fire, do *not* move him before immobilizing. If he must be moved, several people working together will be required (see Chapter 6, "Emergency Transportation") since the head, neck, and spine must be kept in a straight line. Do *not* twist, or bend any part of the neck or spine, as further injury and paralysis could result. One person must hold the head with a slight pull to prevent its being bent forward, backward, or sideways. Two or three others can lift and support the victim. Place on a firm surface such as a door, surfboard, or table; immobilize the head with sleeping bags, rolled-up towels, or pillows, and then strap into position (Fig. 5-3). Then you can transport (see Chapter 6, "Emergency Transportation").

If at any time breathing assistance is necessary, *do not* open the airway by bending the neck as shown in Fig. 3-7. Open the airway by placing your fingers behind the angle of the jaw and pulling forward and holding (Fig. 3-8).

Fig. 5-3: Splinting for head, neck, and spinal injuries

FRACTURE OF THE NOSE: A nose fracture is very common and may result from any hard blow to the nose. If you are backpacking, it is important to treat the broken nose, but immediate medical help is not necessary. Treatment consists of cleaning the outside of the nose gently with soap and water and applying a soft protective compress, such as a gauze pad. Splinting or taping is not necessary but you may straighten the nose if there is obvious deformity. If nasal bleeding occurs, control it by pinching the nostrils together gently and begin your hike back to medical help.

FRACTURE OF THE CHEEKBONE: Fractures of the upper jaw or cheekbone may be suspected if the facial features are distorted, if there is numbness, swelling, bleeding from the nose or mouth, if teeth do not meet normally, or if there is blurring of the vision.

This fracture will require medical attention as soon as possible. Follow the general procedure for all fractures on p. 59, by controlling bleeding and applying a dressing if there are any open wounds. Keep in mind that a fracture of the head may also have occurred.

FRACTURE OF THE LOWER JAW: Severe lower-jaw fractures are painful and deform the face. Such a fracture is likely if the mouth cannot be closed, if blood and saliva drool from the mouth, or if it is painful and difficult to move the jaw and the teeth are uneven. Treatment consists of gently closing the jaw so that the lower teeth rest against the upper ones. Secure the jaw in this position with the use of a 4-tailed bandage (Fig. 5-4 through 5-6) or with 2 folded triangular bandages. Once this is applied, watch the victim closely in case he becomes nauseated and starts to vomit. If this happens, release the bandages at once in order to prevent choking and obstruction of the airway.

Figure 5-4 through 5-6: Splinting for lower-jaw fracture

Fig. 5-4   Fig. 5-5   Fig. 5-6

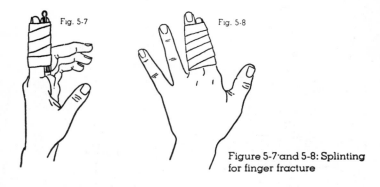

Fig. 5-7   Fig. 5-8

Figure 5-7 and 5-8: Splinting for finger fracture

FRACTURE OF THE FINGER: This is not a serious fracture unless it is accompanied by an open wound. If there is no wound, limit movement of the finger by placing any rigid object under the finger and bandaging it in place (Fig. 5-7). If you do not have any strong object, simply tape the injured finger to the one next to it (Fig. 5-8).

FRACTURE OF THE WRIST OR FOREARM (RADIUS AND ULNA): The two bones in the forearm may be fractured individually or together (the ulna forms the elbow point and joins the outside of the hand; the radius is on the thumb side). In either case, the treatment is the same. You must immediately immobilize the broken bone ends and the adjacent joint by applying any well-padded splint (Fig. 5-9), such as a rolled-up newspaper. Once the broken

Figure 5-9: Splinting for forearm fracture

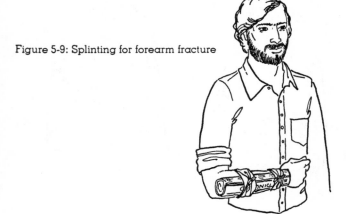

63

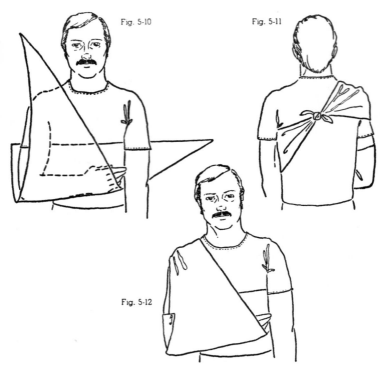

Figure 5-10 through 5-12: Applying an arm sling

Figure 5-13 and 5-14: Splinting for upper-arm fracture

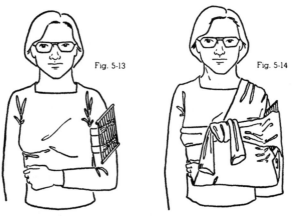

bone ends are splinted, bend the elbow and put the arm in a sling, with the arm slightly raised and the thumb pointing upward (Fig. 5-10 through 5-12).

FRACTURE OF THE UPPER ARM BONE (HUMERUS): When treating a fracture of the upper arm bone, it is extremely important that movement be restricted both at the site of the break and at adjacent joints to minimize damage to muscles, ligaments, and tendons. To do this, splint the fracture securely, using any rigid object (Fig. 5-13). Once the fracture has been splinted, put the arm in a sling (Fig. 5-10 through 5-12) and bind the victim's upper arm to the chest wall (Fig. 5-14).

FRACTURE OF THE SHOULDER BLADE (SCAPULA): A fall may fracture the shoulder blade, most frequently seen in children and older adults. The signs of a broken shoulder blade include pain and swelling on the injured side. An inability to swing the arm of the injured side backward or forward distinguishes this from broken ribs. When treating this fracture, apply an arm sling to eliminate movement at the elbow (Fig. 5-10 through 5-12), and bind the victim's arm to his chest wall (Fig. 5-14).

FRACTURE OF THE COLLARBONE (CLAVICLE): The collarbone usually breaks at the weakest point, about a third of the way from the tip of the shoulder to the breastbone. This fracture is very common in children and will heal without complications in about 3 weeks. Healing for adults takes slightly longer. Treat these fractures as you would a fracture of the shoulder blade.

FRACTURE OF THE RIBS: Broken ribs are characterized by severe pain when the victim breathes deeply and by tenderness over the break area. There may be a depression of the chest if many ribs are fractured in more than one place. If the victim has a punctured lung, he may cough up frothy blood.

Most broken ribs are not serious and may be treated as follows:

1. Have victim breathe as shallowly as possible.

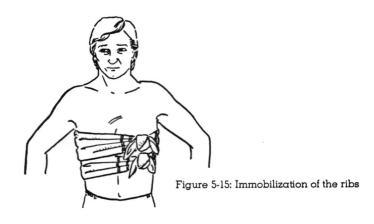

Figure 5-15: Immobilization of the ribs

2. Immobilize the rib cage using a folded triangular bandage or a substitute to help relieve the pain (Fig. 5-15).
3. Make sure the bandage is snug, but not so snug that it interferes with breathing.

If you are in an isolated area and medical help will be delayed, taping the chest in the following way will relieve the pain and allow the victim to walk out with minimum assistance:

1. Apply strips of 3-inch wide adhesive tape horizontally from below the ribs going upward and from the midline of the body in front to the midline in back (Fig. 5-16 and 5-17).
2. Always begin low, to immobilize the lowest ribs first, and then proceed upward.
3. Apply each strip after exhalation, pulling the tape as tightly as can be tolerated.
4. Protect the nipples with gauze in males as well as females. If tape is applied to the chest of a woman with large breasts, run the strips above and below the breasts.

With severe rib fractures, the broken ends of ribs may overlap; the overlapping will look like tines of forks pushing through the skin. Do not strap the chest, but first apply

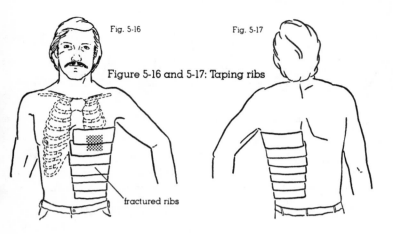

Figure 5-16 and 5-17: Taping ribs

Fig. 5-16   Fig. 5-17

fractured ribs

strips of tape on each side of the fracture and use them to pull the bone ends apart and into proper alignment. This tape will be left on the chest, maintaining the pull. No further taping will be necessary.

If there are multiple broken ribs, if the chest is sunken in, if there are open chest wounds allowing air to escape (see Chapter 7, "Common Emergencies," "Chest Wounds"), or if frothy blood is coming from the victim's mouth, do not carry out the above first-aid fracture treatments as they will only aggravate the existing situation. Try to reach medical assistance as soon as possible.

1. Keep airway open.
2. Treat for shock (see Chapter 2).
3. Encourage the victim to lie on the injured side while waiting for medical assistance.

FRACTURE OF THE PELVIS OR HIP JOINT: Fractures of the pelvis and hip joint are common results of serious falls. You should seek immediate medical help. Meanwhile, carefully roll victim on his back and immobilize by tying the legs together and placing a tie around the hip area. Carefully move him onto any long rigid object, such as a surfboard, picnic-table bench, or cabin door, and then

Figure 5-18: Splinting for pelvis and hip-joint fractures

secure him to this so he cannot move (Fig. 5-18). Anticipate and treat for shock. Once immobilized, he may then be transported with a minimum of movement and pain.

FRACTURE OF THE UPPER LEG BONE (FEMUR): When the upper leg bone is fractured, severe pain and shock follow. This fracture is characterized by a foot that turns outward, a shortened limb, and a distortion of the upper limb due to the overlapped bones and muscle spasm. This type of fracture will require treatment for shock and immediate immobilization of the leg. Do not try to pull the

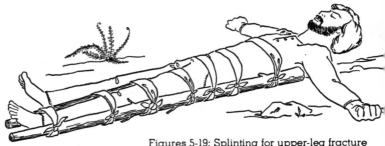

Figures 5-19: Splinting for upper-leg fracture

bones apart to correct the overlapping. Apply two splints for immobilization; the outer splint should be long enough to reach from the victim's armpit to below the heel on the outer side of the injured leg; the inner splint should be long enough to reach from the groin to below the heel on the inner side of the leg. Secure the two splints in place (Fig. 5-19). To transport the victim, see Chapter 6, "Emergency Transportation."

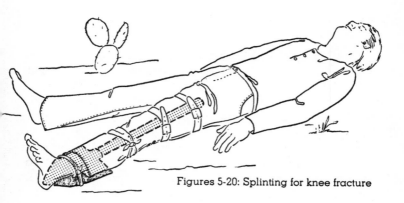

Figures 5-20: Splinting for knee fracture

FRACTURE OF THE KNEECAP (PATELLA): The kneecap, or patella, is in front of the knee joint. It is usually fractured by a direct blow or fall. To decrease pain, immobilize the kneecap and joint immediately. Place a rigid object beneath the knee and bandage it in place, making sure the ties aren't placed directly on kneecap (Fig. 5-20).

FRACTURE OF THE LOWER LEG BONES (TIBIA AND FIBULA): Whether the break is in the tibia (the larger, inner bone, which forms the shin) or fibula or both, the treatment is the same: immediately immobilize the lower leg with rigid splints. Once the splints are in place, fasten

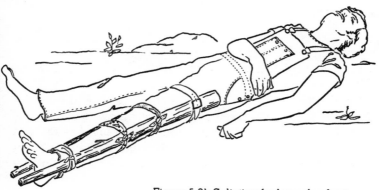

Figure 5-21: Splinting for lower-leg fracture

them tightly to the lower leg and upper leg to eliminate movement at the point of fracture (Fig. 5-21).

FRACTURE OF THE ANKLE: A common cause of injury to the ankle is the severe twisting force caused by stepping into a hole or stumbling on an uneven surface. The victim will complain of pain, swelling, and difficulty in bearing weight on the injured leg. Always treat as a fracture, even though it may be a sprain. Remove his boot, elevate the leg, and apply a heavy, padded splint such as a sleeping bag, jacket, pillow, or blanket. Two bandannas or triangular bandages can be used to fasten the improvised splint in place around the lower leg and foot (Fig. 5-22).

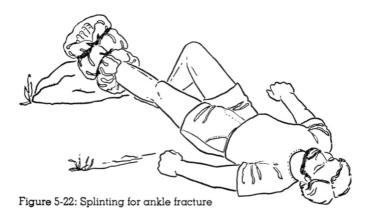

Figure 5-22: Splinting for ankle fracture

DISLOCATIONS

A dislocation is a displacement of the bone end from the joint; it can occur in the shoulder, jaw, elbow, wrist, finger, knee, ankle, or toe. A dislocation usually is the result of a fall or a direct blow applied to the bone. If a joint is dislocated, the bone will not function properly, and the joint will

have an unnatural shape. These signs, coupled with severe pain and immediate swelling, indicate the bone end
is dislocated. When you treat a victim with a dislocation,
you should treat it as you would a closed fracture: splint,
immobilize, elevate, and seek medical help. Never attempt to correct any deformity near a joint or try to replace
the dislocation. While seeking medical help, cold compresses could be applied to reduce blood flow to the site
and thus reduce swelling and pain.

SPRAINS

Tearing or excessive stretching of ligaments, muscles, tendons, and blood vessels around joints results in a sprain.
Sprains are the result of forcing a limb beyond its normal
range of motion. Most often they occur at the ankle but can
also be at the wrist or knee. Early treatment of a sprain is
mainly directed at minimizing swelling and the leakage of
blood into the injured tissue. The sprained joint should be
elevated, rested completely, and treated with cold compresses for the first 24—48 hours. Apply an elastic bandage, using the figure-eight turn (Fig. 1-34), to the affected
part to give additional support and to reduce swelling
while the cold compresses are being applied.

STRAINS

Strains are injuries to muscles from overexertion and are
due to fibers being stretched or partially torn. The back is
the most vulnerable to this injury, and the strain usually
results from improper lifting. Treatment consists of rest,
heat, and the use of a rigid board or other hard surface
under the sleeping bag for firm support. You may also try
hanging by your hands from a low branch, with feet on the
ground and knees slightly bent, so the weight of the back-

side and upper leg stretches the spine, and then rocking to and fro on the heels. Slow walking on level ground may also relieve some of the muscle pain. If the strain is not in the back, treatment is simply heat and rest.

6

Emergency Transportation

Injury or illness becomes an emergency when there is a threat to life, when pain is severe or continuous, or when the victim develops additional physical or emotional problems. If someone in your group develops an acute illness or sustains a serious injury, medical assistance will be necessary. The decision to wait for help, to walk out for help, or to transport the victim yourself will be based upon the seriousness of the injury or illness, the number of people in the party, the distance to civilization, the difficulty of the trail, and/or the availability of a professional rescue service.

There are some injuries after which the victim should never be moved, and which only professional rescue teams with specialized equipment can adequately handle. These are injuries of the head, neck, spinal cord, hip, and pelvis. These victims should be carefully immobilized and then transported. If there is an immediate danger to the victim's life, such as fire, risk of drowning, freezing, or lightning shock, immediate movement of the victim is justified. Take care of the life-threatening problems first and then decide upon the best plan for getting medical assistance for the victim.

There are several ways to signal for help. One way is to build a fire with green leaves and branches to create enough smoke to alert the Forest Service fire spotters. If there is a large open space nearby, spell out SOS or HELP on the ground with clothing or limbs of trees. A signaling mirror may also be used to attract attention.

If there is only one rescuer for a seriously injured or ill victim and there has been no response to the signaling, then the victim may have to be left alone while the rescuer goes for help. This is not recommended, but it may be the only way to obtain medical or paramedical aid.

METHODS OF TRANSPORTATION

There are many methods that can be used to move a victim either to safety or to medical help. As a rescuer, you should review the following techniques and choose the most appropriate one for the type of injury, the distance, and the type of supportive devices and number of rescuers available.

> **It is extremely important to realize that more harm can result from improper transportation of a victim than through any other measures associated with emergency first aid.**

Pulling the Victim

If you must pull or drag a person to safety, pull from one end of the body, preferably the shoulders, but never sideways. Place your hands under the armpits, and support the head with your forearms while you pull (Fig. 6-1). You do not need to lift the victim's shoulders up very far to pull. At no time should you bend or twist any of the body, especially the head, neck, or trunk. The ankle pull (Fig. 6-2) can also be used, but the shoulder pull is preferred since it allows the rescuer to support the head and neck of the victim while pulling.

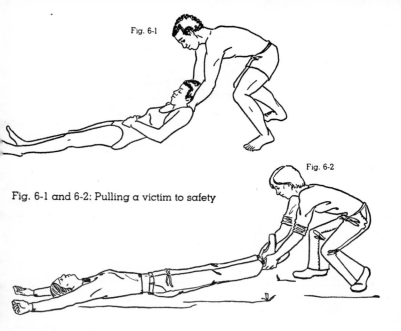

Fig. 6-1

Fig. 6-2

Fig. 6-1 and 6-2: Pulling a victim to safety

Blanket Pull

If an immediate transfer of a victim is needed because of environmental hazards, a blanket can also be used to pull, lift, or carry him short distances to safety. The rescuer places the blanket down along one side of the victim. He then accordion-folds the blanket toward the victim's side in six-inch-wide pleats, tucking it close to the victim. Accordion-folding the blanket into a narrow strip will make it easier to place the victim on the blanket and to pull it under him with the least amount of movement (Fig. 6-3 through 6-6). Once the blanket is under the victim, he can then be covered to maintain his body temperature. The weight of the victim will keep him on the blanket for short distance pulls. If there are four or more rescuers, they can carry the victim on the blanket for a short distance. This method is not meant for long distances.

If you suspect a spinal fracture or head injury and quick removal from hazard is necessary, one rescuer should

PLACING BLANKET UNDER VICTIM FOR BLANKET DRAG

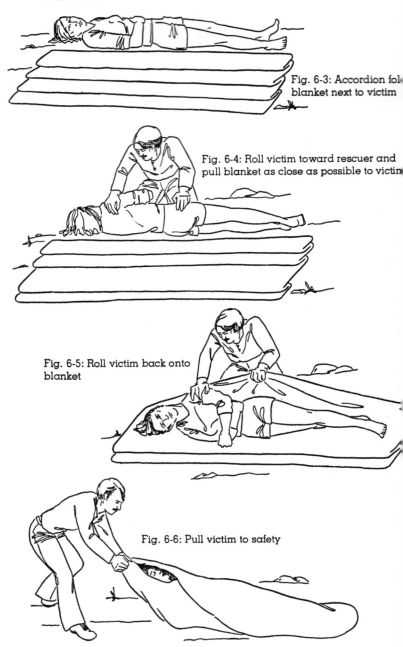

Fig. 6-3: Accordion fold blanket next to victim

Fig. 6-4: Roll victim toward rescuer and pull blanket as close as possible to victim

Fig. 6-5: Roll victim back onto blanket

Fig. 6-6: Pull victim to safety

support the head and neck while the other turns the victim onto his side, pulls the blanket up to the victim, and then rolls him back on to the blanket. If there is only one rescuer, the shoulder pull may be the only way to move the victim away from danger.

Remember: move the victim as a unit. Do not permit any twisting, bending, or side-to-side motion of the head, neck, or spine (see Chapter 5 "Bone and Muscle Injuries" for "Fractures of the Head, Neck, or Spine"). Do not use the blanket to lift or carry a victim with suspected fracture of the head, neck, or spine unless there is an immediate need for removal from danger. You should use something more rigid (see Fig. 5-18).

Lifting the Victim

If the victim is lightweight and has no serious wounds or skeletal injuries, he may be carried by one person. Simply place one hand under his knees and the other around his upper back and transport him to safety (Fig. 6-7).

Fig. 6-7: Lifting the victim

Fig. 6-8   Fig. 6-9

Fig. 6-8 and 6-9: Assisting the victim to safety

Supporting the Victim

If the victim is conscious and has no serious wounds or skeletal injuries, he may be assisted to walk to safety. Begin this technique by helping the victim to his feet. Place one of his arms around your neck and hold his hand at your shoulder. Place your other arm about his waist for additional support (Fig. 6-8). Two rescuers can use this technique together (Fig. 6-9).

Fig. 6-10: Fore-and-aft carry

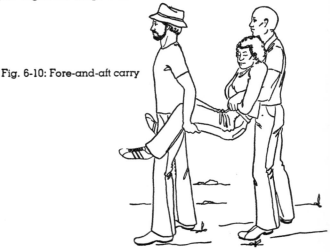

Fore-and-Aft Carry

The fore-and-aft carry requires two rescuers. It may be used to move an unconscious victim to safety or to medical help, but it should not be used when there are serious injuries to the trunk, head, or neck, or when there may be fractures (Fig. 6-10). When carrying the victim in this way, make sure you do not close off his airway; be especially careful if the victim is unconscious.

Two-Handed Seat Carry

If the victim does not have serious injuries and is conscious, two rescuers can move him in a two-hand seat carry (Fig. 6-11 through 6-13). The victim should place his arms about the shoulders of both rescuers to provide additional support to the lift.

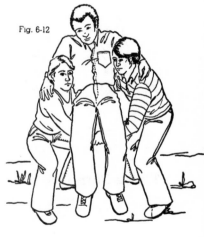

Fig. 6-11

Fig. 6-12

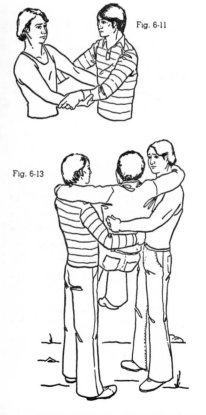

Fig. 6-13

Fig. 6-11 through 6-13:
Two-handed seat carry

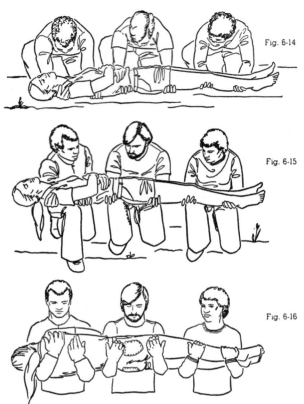

Fig. 6-14

Fig. 6-15

Fig. 6-16

Fig. 6-14 through 6-16: Three-man lift

Three-Man Lift

Three rescuers are needed for the three-man lift. This lift is useful when the victim can only be approached from one side. The rescuers are evenly dispersed at the victim's side, one at the shoulder, one at the hips, and one at the knees. Each rescuer kneels on his knee that is closest to the victim's feet and then all simultaneously place their hands under the victim (Fig. 6-14). The person at the head of the victim gives simple commands to ensure that all the rescuers lift together; this will minimize the possibility of the rescuers' losing their balance during the lift. The command "Prepare to lift" followed by "Lift" will raise the victim to the rescuers' knees (Fig. 6-15). Make sure the victim's body is kept in a straight line. This is followed by "Prepare to stand" and "Stand." The victim should now be rolled toward the rescuers' chests; this position is easier for the rescuers to hold, and will give a sense of security to the victim (Fig. 6-16). To lower the victim, the reverse procedure is used.

Three-Man Hammock Carry

The three-man hammock carry can be used whether the victim is lying on his face or back. This technique could be

Fig. 6-17 through 6-20: Three-man hammock carry

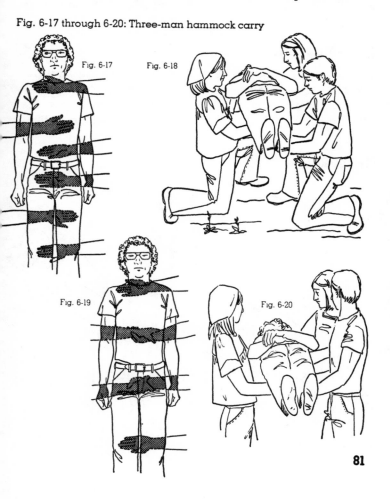

Fig. 6-17   Fig. 6-18

Fig. 6-19   Fig. 6-20

used to move and carry a victim to safety or medical help. The hammock carry is easiest for walking and carrying the victim at the same time. Two rescuers kneel on one side of the victim and one rescuer on the other, placing their hands beneath the victim (Fig. 6-17). The rescuer at the head of the victim gives the command "Prepare to lift" followed by "Lift," when the victim is lifted to the rescuers' knees (Fig. 6-18) and rested there while their hands are slid far enough under the victim to secure two interlocking grips with rescuer on the opposite side (Fig. 6-19). The final phase of the lift is "Prepare to stand" and "Stand" (Fig. 6-20). The victim is now in a position to be transported. To lower the victim, reverse the procedure.

One-Man Back Carry

The one-man back carry is valuable if the victim's injuries are not too serious and he weighs no more than the rescuer. If the victim is unconscious and cannot help in the lift, you must lie down with your back against the victim's

Fig. 6-21 through 6-23: One-man back carry

Fig. 6-21

Fig. 6-22

Fig. 6-23

chest. In this position, bring the victim's arm over your shoulder and place it next to your chest. Grasp the victim's clothing and roll him over onto your back (Fig. 6-21). Once the victim is on your back, get to both knees (Fig. 6-22), then to one knee, and finally to a standing position (Fig. 6-23).

Improvised Litter

In emergencies with no professional rescue personnel or in remote areas where litters are not available, a stretcher or litter may be improvised to transport a victim to medical help. Use two very sturdy poles or branches and a blanket, tarpaulin, or a sleeping bag. Fold tarpaulin over poles as shown in Fig. 6-24 and Fig. 6-25. The victim's weight on 3 layers of blanket or tarpaulin will hold the litter together and will support the victim. The victim can be placed on

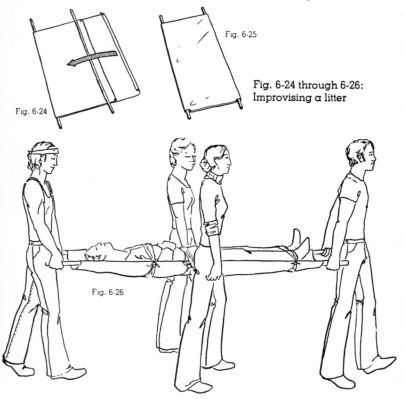

Fig. 6-25

Fig. 6-24 through 6-26:
Improvising a litter

Fig. 6-24

Fig. 6-26

the improvised litter using a shoulder (Fig. 6-1) or blanket pull (Fig. 6-6), the 3-man lift (Fig. 6-16) or the 3-man hammock carry (Fig. 6-20). If the victim has splinted fractures, careful handling is necessary to transfer him to a litter. Secure him in place as seen in Fig. 6-26, so he will not roll or slide.

When transporting a victim, do not march in step; if you do, you will swing the victim and run the risk of complicating his injuries by the additional movement (Fig. 6-26).

7

Common Emergencies

ABDOMINAL PAIN

(see also Appendicitis; Miscarriage)

SYMPTOMS: Pain in the upper part of the abdomen or stomach; common in simple indigestion, overeating, and eating while emotionally upset. Cramping pain in the lower part of the abdomen is common in viral infections or diarrhea. If the pain becomes continuous and is aggravated by walking, eating, coughing, or straining; if the abdomen is tender to touch or is hard; and if this is accompanied by nausea and vomiting, diarrhea and fever, then the symptoms may indicate a more serious condition and will require medical attention as soon as it can be obtained. Usually the symptoms do not develop into an emergency and will settle down in a couple of hours.

CAUSE: Indigestion, food or plant poisoning, appendicitis, miscarriage, internal bleeding.

TREATMENT:
1. Keep victim quiet.
2. Place him in shock position (Fig. 2-3).

3. Cover if necessary to maintain body temperature.
4. Get medical assistance without delay, if pain continues.

Do not give a laxative.
Do not give an enema.
Do not give any food or liquids.
Do not give any medication for pain.
Do not apply heat or cold to the abdomen.

ABRASIONS AND MINOR CUTS

(see also Chapter 1, "Wounds and Bleeding")

SYMPTOMS: Scraped skin; oozing or bleeding from the scraped skin.

TREATMENT:
1. Thoroughly scrub with plain soap and water to remove foreign material. Hydrogen peroxide may be used to clean.
2. Dry the abrasion or cut.
3. Apply an antiseptic ointment.
4. If further contamination is likely as you continue your backpacking, cover lightly with a nonadherent dressing, such as a Telfa pad.

ALLERGIC REACTIONS

(see also "Poisoning by Insects" in Chapter 4)

SYMPTOMS: Apprehension; flushing; itching or burning; hives; sneezing or coughing; respiratory difficulty; wheezing and shortness of breath; hoarseness; bluish skin color (cyanosis); pallor, weak pulse.

CAUSES: Individualized allergic responses to foreign proteins such as shellfish, multiple insect bites, penicillin or other drugs.

TREATMENT:
1. Check for a Medic Alert tag or other identifying card.
2. Give antihistamine drug if available.
3. Ensure adequate airway (Fig. 3-7).
4. Start artificial respiration (Chapter 3) if breathing becomes difficult or impossible due to swelling of the throat. Start CPR (Chapter 3) if the heart stops beating.
5. Treat victim for shock (Chapter 2).
6. Transport to medical facility immediately.

PREVENTION: If you have a history of severe allergic reactions, carry a kit with you that will include adrenaline and a syringe for administration. Tell another member of the group where the kit is in your pack and what to do if you are unable to give yourself the injection.

ALTITUDE SICKNESS

SYMPTOMS: Drowsiness; headache; lethargy; reduced night vision; impaired judgment and memory; euphoria; nausea and vomiting; eventual loss of consciousness.

CAUSE: Rapid rise to a higher altitude.

TREATMENT:
1. Reduce activity for 2 – 3 days.
2. If no change, return to a lower altitude.

PREVENTION: Plan your ascent so that it will be gradual and allow rests and stopover time.

APPENDICITIS

(see also Abdominal Pain)

SYMPTOMS: Loss of appetite; nausea and vomiting; severe abdominal pains; extreme tenderness in the lower right abdomen lasting more than a few hours; a slight fever. You may test for appendicitis by slowly and gently compressing the wall of the abdomen inward and then releasing it suddenly. Sharp pain as the abdomen is released indicates irritation of the lining of the abdominal cavity.

CAUSE: Inflammation or rupture of the appendix.

TREATMENT:

1. No body activity.
2. Position victim in the way he will be most comfortable. Shock position (Fig. 2-1 through Fig. 2-3) is always a safe position if cause of pain is not known.
3. Cover if necessary to maintain body temperature.
4. Get medical assistance without delay.

Do not give a laxative.
Do not give an enema.
Do not give any food or liquids.
Do not give any medication for pain.
Do not apply heat or cold to the abdomen.

BLADDER INFECTION

SYMPTOMS: Frequency and urgency of urination; burning with urination; lower abdominal pain; cloudy urine.

CAUSES: Inadequate intake of fluid; dehydration; inadequate cleansing of the genital area; injury to urethra (opening from bladder); obstruction of the urethra.

1. Force fluids—at least 2 glasses every hour.
2. Reduce activity.
3. Warm sitz bath if possible; that is, sit in a tub or pan of warm water for 20 minutes at a time until relieved.
4. If symptoms are not relieved by the above in 24 hours, then medical assistance is necessary.

PREVENTION: If this is a condition you have had before, remember to keep well hydrated and to continue good personal hygiene even though it may be difficult in primitive areas. If you have a prescription for an anti-infective such as Gantrisin, bring it along. You can start taking the medication at the first symptom of a bladder infection.

BLISTERS

SYMPTOMS: A "hot spot" sensation; redness; tenderness; swelling with fluid, either water or blood.

CAUSES: Friction and pressure from shoes or boots, ropes, backpack straps; pinching; hitting; burns.

TREATMENT:

1. If the friction or pressure on the blister can be removed, it is best to leave the blister unbroken until it dries.
2. Wash the entire area carefully with antiseptic or plain soap and water and then dry.
3. If the blister cannot be exposed to the air to dry, then the fluid may be removed in the following way.
   a. Sterilize a needle with a flame or soak it in alcohol for 20 minutes.
   b. Puncture the lower edge of the blister and drain (Fig. 7-1).
4. Apply a sterile nonadherent dressing, such as a Telfa pad.
5. If the blister breaks before you can stop to take care of it, treat it as an open wound (see Abrasions and Minor Cuts).

PREVENTION: Blisters are the number-one problem of hikers. Only a few simple measures are necessary for prevention. The most important of these is making sure your boots are completely broken in, well fitting, and contoured to your feet. Each time you stop to rest, take off your boots; change to a clean pair of socks at midday; and whenever possible, rest your feet by wearing tennis shoes. Moleskin or molefoam is effective in preventing blisters. Apply patches to those areas of your feet, such as the heels, ankles, and toes, that you know will rub in the boot.

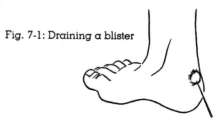

Fig. 7-1: Draining a blister

BOILS

SYMPTOMS: Tenderness; pain; raised hard area with a yellow or black center, usually on the back of the neck, in the armpits, or on the buttocks.

CAUSES: Irritation; pressure; friction; excessive perspiration.

TREATMENT:

1. Protect area from irritation, squeezing, and trauma. Be very careful of boils on the face, as infection could spread to the brain.
2. Apply hot, wet compresses.
3. Apply an antiseptic ointment.

BURNS

(see also Eye Injuries)

SYMPTOMS: Grouped according to the degree of burn in terms of depth and of tissue destruction, as well as the amount of body area affected.

   First Degree: affects only the outer layer of skin and produces pain, tingling, redness but no blistering (Fig. 7-2). Remember that even first-degree burns can be life threatening if a large area of the body is involved, as in a sunburn.

Fig. 7-2 through 7-4: First-, second-, and third-degree burns

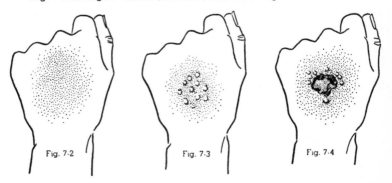

Second Degree: involves a greater thickness of the skin, which will be blistered, mottled red, swollen, and very painful (Fig. 7-3).

Third Degree: involves full thickness of the skin and deeper tissues and appears dry, pale, white, or charred, with little or no pain (Fig. 7-4).

CAUSES: Burns are injuries to the tissues caused by *thermal agents* (fire, cold, radiation, hot objects, hot fluids, sun), *electrical agents* (lightning, electricity), and *chemical agents* (acids, strong alkalis, gasoline, butane, smoke).

TREATMENT:

Major Thermal and Electrical Burns:

1. Put out any fire by smothering it or drowning it with water.
2. Immediately remove smoldering garments or fragments of clothing, belts, buckles, shoes and jewelry (swelling may make later removal impossible). Synthetics may stick to the burn, so do not try to remove.
3. Cool burned surfaces immediately by applying cool wet towels or by immersing in cold water.
4. Maintain open airway (Fig. 3-7). Watch for difficulty in breathing!
5. Check for other injuries and treat in order of priority (see Chapter 2, "Shock").
6. Treat for shock (Chapter 2).
7. Give Cardiopulmonary Resuscitation if needed (Chapter 3).
8. Keep victim at rest.
9. Elevate burned extremities.
10. Cover the burned areas with as clean a material as possible.
11. Maintain victim's body temperature; avoid chilling and cover with blankets that will not stick to the burns.
12. Do not use any ointments or salves.
13. Do not break any blisters.
14. Transport victim to a medical facility as soon as possible.

Minor Thermal Burns:

1. Wash your hands well with soap and water.
2. Remove any clothing over the wound; cut away if necessary.
3. Immediately rinse well with cold water for 10 minutes at a time or apply a continuous cool, moist pack to the burn.
4. Burn may be washed gently with a mild soap and warm water after the cold pack.
5. Cover wound with a sterile, nonadherent dressing.
6. Wrap with a clean bandage or bandanna for comfort and protection from the environment.
7. A mild analgesic such as aspirin may be necessary.

Chemical Burns:

1. Immediately irrigate the area with a continuous and copious stream of water or a mixture of 1 teaspoon of baking soda to a pint of water.
2. If a large part of the body surface is involved, immersion in a stream or lake may be easier and more efficient.
3. Continue to flood the area of the burn while removing the clothing.
4. After thorough washing, follow the first-aid directions for Major Thermal and Electrical Burns.

CHEST PAIN

(see also Heart Attack)

SYMPTOMS: Strong pain in the chest area.

CAUSES: Food poisoning; ulcers; gallbladder attack; heart attack; angina; severe muscular strain; pneumonia; upper respiratory infection.

TREATMENT:

1. Have victim remain quiet in position of comfort.
2. As soon as possible, transport to medical assistance if pain is not relieved.
3. Initiate Cardiopulmonary Resuscitation if needed (Chapter 3).

CHEST WOUNDS, SUCKING WOUNDS

SYMPTOMS: Audible passing of air in and out of the chest wound during breathing; wheezing; bluish skin color (cyanosis); difficulty in breathing; chest pain; anxious expression.

CAUSES: Penetration of the rib cage and lung by a sharp instrument such as a knife, bullet, sharp stick.

TREATMENT:

1. You will need a dressing to prevent air from passing through the puncture; it could consist of a very wet cloth, Vaseline spread heavily on a clean piece of material, a plastic bag, a piece of plastic wrap, or aluminum foil.
2. Have victim exhale and hold.
3. Quickly cover the wound at entry and exit if present with the air-proof dressing. Victim may then inhale (Fig. 7-5).
4. Apply a pressure dressing as seen in Fig. 5-15.
5. Treat for shock (Chapter 2).
6. Transport to a medical facility.

Do not probe for the foreign object or attempt to remove a protruding object.

Do not administer any narcotic, as it may slow down the respiration.

Do not give the victim anything to drink or eat.

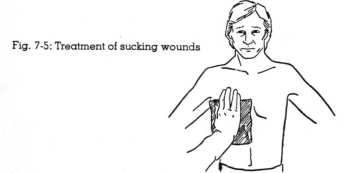

Fig. 7-5: Treatment of sucking wounds

CHILBLAINS

(see Cold Injuries)

CHOKING

*(see also Chapter 3, "Choking,
Respiratory, and Circulatory Emergencies.")*

SYMPTOMS: Wheezing sound when breathing; unable to speak; hand clutching throat; bluish skin color.
CAUSES: Large, poorly chewed portions of food; elevated blood-alcohol level; foreign objects, such as dentures.

> **Do not interfere with victim's attempt to expel the foreign body or obstruction.**
> **Do not ask the victim what is wrong.**

TREATMENT:
1. Remove obstruction by administering several sharp blows between the shoulder blades (Fig. 3-1).
2. If object is still lodged, administer four manual thrusts—either abdominal or chest thrusts (Fig. 3-2 through 3-5).
3. If object is still lodged, repeat steps 1 and 2.
4. Once obstruction is removed, give artificial respiration (Chapter 3) if victim is not breathing.

COLD INJURIES: CHILBLAINS, FROSTBITE, HYPOTHERMIA

(see also Snow Blindness)

SYMPTOMS:

Chilblains: redness; swelling; burning; itching.

Frostbite: to hands, feet, nose, ears: uncomfortable feeling of severe cold; aching sensation; the skin looks red, it may tingle and then become numb. If exposure continues, blisters may form, and the area of frostbite swells and feels hard. In more severe cases of exposure, or if first-aid treatment is not given, the skin may turn white, gray, or waxy yellow, and become free of pain, indicating deep tissue damage.

CAUSES: Combinations of low temperature, low humidity, wind, prolonged exposure, and lack of proper clothing.

TREATMENT:

Chilblains:

1. Check for and then cover any exposed area of the body.
2. Reduce activity while symptoms are present.
3. Drink warm fluids.

Frostbite:

1. Do not allow the victim to walk if legs or feet are frostbitten.
2. Transport to a protective shelter. Frostbitten hands may be placed in the armpits or between the legs for warmth even before removing victim to shelter.
3. Remove constrictive clothing.
4. Rewarm frostbitten extremity rapidly by immersing it in tepid water.
5. Handle part gently and protect it from further injury.
6. Elevate extremity.
7. Provide for general body warmth, warm liquids, rest, and sleep.

Do not rub the frostbitten part; this causes crystallized fluid to damage tissue.

Do not rub with snow or soak in cold water.

Do not expose to open fire; the tissue is more sensitive to heat.

Victim should not smoke; this will constrict blood vessels and reduce circulation.

Hypothermia:

1. Get victim out of the wind and rain.
2. Take off all wet clothes and put on dry ones.
3. Get victim into a warm sleeping bag—it may be warmed with hot stones from the fire.
4. Give him something warm to drink.
5. Try to keep the victim awake, exercising if possible.

6. If the shivering doesn't stop, take all the victim's clothes off and put him into a sleeping bag with another stripped person. Body warmth is the best treatment.

7. Have him rest overnight after recovery.

PREVENTION: Try to save your body heat in every way possible. The wind-chill factor must be considered, since both wind and environmental temperature will affect the rate of heat loss. Wear protective clothing that consists of several layers of cloth with air spaces between to serve as insulation. The outer layer should be windproof and water-repellent. Wear wool socks over lightweight cotton socks plus your heavy, water-repellent shoes or boots. Mittens keep hands warmer than gloves. All clothing must fit without constricting any part of the body. Remember that bare head, legs, and hands increase body heat loss, which in turn increases your energy requirements.

Stay dry. Perspiration trapped in your clothes will conduct heat away from your body as much as a cold rain.

If you are tired as well as wet, the environmental temperature does not have to be below freezing for you to suffer from hypothermia. Stop at intervals to rest and to snack on some high-energy food. Set up the camp before you are exhausted; get out of the wind and the rain. You don't have to reach your goal every day!

COMMON COLD

(see Upper Respiratory Infections)

CONTACT LENS REMOVAL

(see also Eye Injuries)

Someone who is unconscious or who has a serious injury should have his contact lenses removed, since prolonged contact of the cornea with the lens will cause corneal damage.

To look for a contact lens, gently separate the eyelids and shine a small light into the eye from the side. Small corneal lenses, the most widely used, are smaller than the colored part of the eye, the iris. A few people wear the larger scleral lenses, which cover all the iris and some of the white.

Do not try to remove a contact lens if the cornea of the eye is not visible upon opening the eyelids.
Do not use force to remove a contact lens.
Do not attempt to remove a contact lens from an injured eye.

CORNEAL LENS REMOVAL:

1. Wash your hands thoroughly before examining the eye.
2. For the right eye, kneel on the right side of the victim.
3. Lightly place your left thumb on the upper eyelid, right thumb on the lower eyelid close to the edge (Fig. 7-6).
4. Gently pull the lids apart. Do not apply pressure directly on the eye (Fig. 7-7).

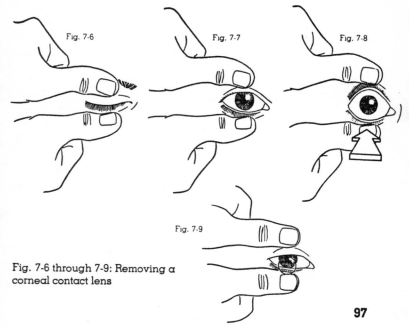

Fig. 7-6   Fig. 7-7   Fig. 7-8

Fig. 7-9

Fig. 7-6 through 7-9: Removing a corneal contact lens

5. If the lens is visible, it should slide easily with the movement of the eyelids while your thumbs are still on the eyelid edges. The lens must be over the cornea if it is to be safely removed.

6. Gently open the lids wider beyond the top and bottom edges of the lens and hold.

7. Press gently downward with right thumb on the eyeball (Fig. 7-8). The lens should tip up on one edge.

8. Then slide the eyelids and thumbs together gently (Fig. 7-9) with slightly more pressure on the lower eyelid. This should cause the contact lens to slip out from between the lids, where it can be retrieved.

9. Move to the left side of the victim and repeat.

10. Place lenses in containers marked Left and Right.

SCLERAL LENS REMOVAL:

1. Wash hands thoroughly.

2. For the right eye, stand or kneel by the victim's right side.

3. Place left index finger parallel with and at the edge of the lower eyelid (Fig. 7-10).

4. Press the lid downward and backward until the edge of the scleral lens becomes visible (Fig. 7-11).

5. Maintain pressure but pull finger with lower lid toward victim's right ear (Fig. 7-12). This should cause the lid to slide under the lens. Avoid forcing the lens.

6. Grasp scleral lens with right finger and thumb.

7. Repeat for left.

8. Place lenses in marked containers.

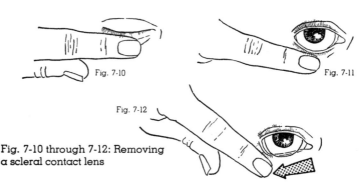

Fig. 7-10

Fig. 7-11

Fig. 7-12

Fig. 7-10 through 7-12: Removing a scleral contact lens

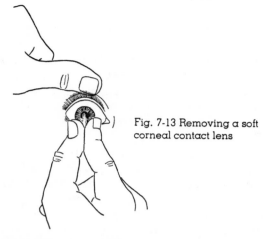

Fig. 7-13 Removing a soft corneal contact lens

SOFT CORNEAL LENS REMOVAL: The soft corneal lenses are about the same size as the scleral lenses, but are very flexible. They must move freely on the eyes. If they do not, drop sterile saline solution or sterile water, several drops at a time, into the eyes before trying to remove them. The lenses could stick to the surface, and removal would damage the cornea.

1. Wash hands thoroughly.
2. Raise the upper lid with the thumb of one hand.
3. Pinch the lens with the thumb and first finger of the other hand (Fig. 7-13). The lens should respond easily, being very flexible.
4. Put lenses in marked containers.

CONVULSIONS (SEIZURE; FIT)

(see also Heat Stroke; Fever; Insulin Shock;
Chapter 4, "Poisoning")

SYMPTOMS: Victim may cry out and fall down; loss of consciousness; stiffness of extremities and neck followed by uncontrollable muscular movements or twitching; rolling back of the eyes; excessive salivation; guttural sounds; blood from the mouth if the tongue is bitten; bluish skin color (cyanosis); absence of breathing; involuntary urination and bowel movement.

CAUSES: High fever; heat stroke; brain hemorrhage; head injuries; drugs; acute infections; insulin shock (hypoglycemia); epilepsy; acute poisoning; alcoholic or drug withdrawal; overrapid breathing (hyperventilation); brain tumor.

TREATMENT:

1. If there is a warning, ease victim to the ground and slip something under his head to prevent head injury.
2. Following the seizure, turn victim on his side to allow for drainage of saliva and to open the airway.
3. Loosen all constrictive clothing.
4. Victim may sleep soundly for a variable time and have no memory of the episode when he awakens.
5. If the convulsion is due to a high fever, remove all clothing, sponge the entire body with cool water, and administer aspirin. Transport to a medical facility for further treatment if fever does not come down and convulsions continue.

Do not attempt to hold victim down during the convulsion. Do not try to place any protective object between his teeth *during* a convulsion. If there is a warning, insert a folded handkerchief between the teeth to protect cheek and tongue.

PREVENTION: Let someone in the group know if you or a member of the group have epilepsy and must take medications daily. Carry more than enough of the required medications, in case you are gone longer than expected.

CROUP

(see Upper Respiratory Infections)

CUTS

(see Abrasions and Minor Cuts; Chapter 1, "Wounds and Bleeding")

DEHYDRATION

SYMPTOMS: Fever; dry skin; dry mouth; difficult breathing; nausea; muscle cramps.

CAUSES Inadequate fluids; high environmental temperatures.

TREATMENT:
1. Administer water, juices.
2. Rest until symptoms subside.

DIABETIC COMA (HYPERGLYCEMIA)

(see also Insulin Shock)

SYMPTOMS: Flushed face; thirst; headache; nausea and vomiting; hot and dry skin; lethargy; drowsiness; abdominal pain; very deep, rapid breathing; rapid pulse; fruity odor to the breath; loss of consciousness.

CAUSES: Insufficient insulin or failure to take it; not following the diabetic diet; infection, vomiting, diarrhea, or injuries could contribute to the development of diabetic coma.

TREATMENT OF EARLY SYMPTOMS OF DIABETIC COMA: (before unconsciousness develops)
1. If a person in the group is familiar with the symptoms and can recognize them before coma develops, he can alert the diabetic to take his insulin, or he can give him some based upon instructions from the diabetic.
2. Keep the victim warm and at rest.
3. If the victim is able to swallow, give him fluids made up of 1 teaspoon of salt (1 salt tablet) and ½ teaspoon of baking soda to each quart of water.
4. If infection, vomiting, diarrhea, or injuries are contributing to the victim's insulin imbalance, then further treatment at a medical facility will be needed.

TREATMENT FOR DIABETIC COMA:
1. This will require medical treatment of intravenous

fluids and insulin. There is no way of knowing how much insulin to give without instructions from the victim, or without specific laboratory tests.

2. Transport to medical facility.

PREVENTION: If you or any member of your group is diabetic, it would be wise to inform someone else. Let them know what to do should insulin be required and how to identify the signs of impending diabetic coma or insulin shock. Show them where the injection kit will be and teach them to draw up and administer the necessary medications.

DIARRHEA

(see also "Ingested Poisons" in Chapter 4)

SYMPTOMS: Abdominal cramping; watery or bloody bowel movements; weakness; dehydration; fever; nausea and vomiting; shock.

CAUSES: Water or food poisoning; viral gastroenteritis; intestinal allergy; antibiotics; psychological stress such as fear or shock.

TREATMENT:

1. Keep victim at rest.
2. If victim is not vomiting, encourage drinking of boiled water or weak tea.
3. Do not offer food.
4. Give Lomotil or Kaopectate after each bowel movement, but only up to 3 doses in 24 hours.
5. Maintain body temperature.
6. If diarrhea persists, seek medical assistance.

PREVENTION: Do not eat any unkown substance. Boil drinking water for at least 10 minutes if it may be contaminated.

DROWNING

CAUSES: Aspiration of water into the lungs; an obstruc-

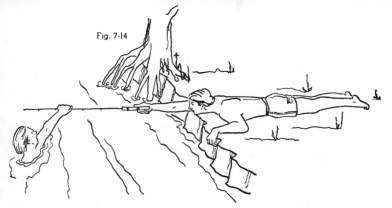

Fig. 7-14 and 7-15: Assisting a drowning victim

Fig. 7-15

tion of the airway due to an involuntary spasm of the larynx while in the water.

RESCUE:

1. Do not attempt bodily contact with the victim unless you have had an American Red Cross Lifesaving course. A drowning person is panicked; he may drown you.

2. If the victim is near the shore or if you can wade out to him, hold out a towel, branch, or fishing pole or throw out a rope for him to grab and then pull him in (Fig. 7-14). If you are a swimmer, go to victim and hand him one of the suggested objects, and then pull him in.

3. If a boat or canoe is available, row out, extend the oar or paddle out over the end of the boat, have him grab onto it (Fig. 7-15), and then pull him up to the end of the boat. He can hold on there while you row back to shore. If he can't hold on, check him for other injuries, and then carefully pull him into the boat.

4. If the drowning victim loses consciousness and sinks down into the water, the nonswimmer should not attempt rescue. Leave it to the experienced swimmer and lifesaver.

TREATMENT FOR REVIVING A DROWNING VICTIM:

1. Begin artificial respiration as soon after rescue as you can. Start artificial respiration in the water, if it can be done without endangering yourself.
2. Inflate the lungs with 10 quick breaths initially.
3. Blow forcefully into the victim in order to push the air through the water in the air passages.
4. Be aware that there may be spinal or neck injuries (see Fig. 3-8).
5. Maintain the open airway (Fig. 3-7).
6. If air is in the stomach, and if there are no spinal or neck injuries, turn head to one side and press firmly on the stomach (Fig. 3-12).
7. Maintain artificial respiration as long as you can or until the victim starts to breathe on his own.
8. Treat for shock and transport to a medical facility.

Do not waste time trying to remove water from the lungs; water cannot be poured from the lungs.

PREVENTION:

1. Learn to swim.
2. Never swim alone.
3. Do not swim if you are exhausted or if the water is very cold.
4. If your boat overturns, stay with it. It will keep you afloat until rescue.
5. Check the depth of the water before you dive into it.

EARACHE

SYMPTOMS: Severe pain in the ear; dizziness; hearing loss; fever.

CAUSES: Infection; allergy; rapid change in the altitude;

swimming in contaminated water; foreign body in the ear such as an insect.

TREATMENT:
1. Apply warm compresses to the external ear.
2. Give pain medication such as aspirin.
3. If fever develops and persists, medical help will be necessary to provide antibiotic therapy.
4. If an insect is in the ear, mineral oil or cooking oil dropped into the ear will smother the insect and it will float out.

PREVENTION: Avoid putting anything into the external ear. Avoid vigorous blowing of your nose during an upper respiratory infection. Use ear plugs while swimming if you are prone to ear infections. If you scuba or snorkel, dry your ears well after each immersion. Do not irrigate your ears.

EPILEPSY

(see Convulsions)

EYE INJURIES

(see also Contact Lens Removal; Snow Blindness)

In general, when an eye is injured, it is best to treat the victim, but leave the eye alone. The exception to this rule is a chemical injury to the eye. Chemical burns of the eye due to acids, poisons, and alkalis need *immediate*, *prolonged* irrigation.

Eye injuries may involve the lids and soft tissues around the eyes, the surface of the eyeball, or the eye itself. Injuries of the surface or deeper structures of the eye are most serious as they may lead to impaired vision or loss of sight. Treatments will require the assistance of a camping buddy.

SYMPTOMS: Pain in the eye; excessive tearing; discharge; bruising around the eye; scratchy feeling; inability to open eye; redness of the eye

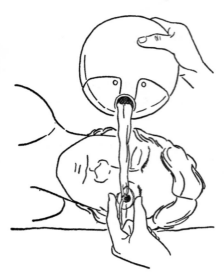

Fig. 7-16: Irrigating the eye

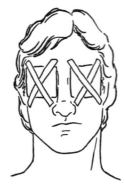

Fig. 7-17: Eye covering

CAUSES: Chemical burns; thermal burns associated with face or body burns; foreign bodies; impaling upon a sharp object; blow to the eye

TREATMENT:

Chemical Burns:

1. Immediately irrigate the eye with generous amounts of water, beer, or carbonated beverage (Fig. 7-16), but preferably water, if available. Hold eyelids open to allow the stream of water to wash out the chemical. Irrigate for at least 10 minutes, pouring slowly.
2. Repeat every 15 – 20 minutes until transported to nearest emergency facility.
3. Cover both eyes when not irrigating to reduce pain and keep eyes at rest (Fig. 7-17).

Thermal Burns:

1. Cover both eyes; protect from contamination (Fig. 7-17).
2. Apply cold compresses to the eyes.
3. Seek medical help.
4. You may offer pain medication, such as aspirin.

Foreign Bodies:

Do not rub the eye or pick at it if there is a scratch or foreign body on the cornea of the eye.
Never put medications of any kind into an injured eye without a physician's order.

1. Wash eye out with water (Fig. 7-16).
2. When removing foreign particles from the eye, do not touch the cornea.
3. Have the injured person lie down and face the sky.
4. If the foreign body can be seen, remove it with the twisted corner of a *clean* piece of cloth (Fig. 7-18). Do not use absorbent cotton balls or a Q-tip.
5. If the object cannot be seen, try to wash out the foreign body by pulling upper lid down over the lower lid while victim looks down. Tearing may assist in the washing out of the object.
6. If this doesn't work, then examine the inner surface of the upper lid by the following method.
   a. Grasp the upper eyelashes and pull down at the same time. Place matchstick or Q-tip above lid (Fig. 7-19).

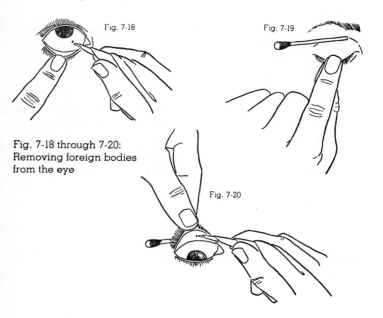

Fig. 7-18

Fig. 7-19

Fig. 7-18 through 7-20:
Removing foreign bodies
from the eye

Fig. 7-20

    b. Roll the upper lid over the matchstick and fold eyelid back on itself (Fig. 7-20).

    c. Remove object with the tip of a clean cloth.

7. Have the victim wear sunglasses for at least one day after removal.

Eyeball Penetration: No matter how superficial the injury, if the pupils appear dissimilar or if the eyeball appears to be altered in shape, you must consider this a very serious injury and provide immediate medical care.

1. Bandage both eyes lightly with a sterile dressing (Fig. 7-17), but do not apply pressure with it.
2. Keep victim at rest as much as possible.
3. Stay with him to reduce anxiety.
4. Transport him carefully to medical aid and an eye specialist.

Do not touch wounds penetrating the eyeball.
Do not attempt to withdraw any foreign object puncturing the eye.
Do not apply pressure to an eye or eyelid to stop bleeding. Let it bleed. If you apply enough pressure to stop the bleeding, you may injure the eye.

Black Eye:
1. Apply cold compresses intermittently for the first 24 hours to control swelling.
2. Apply warm compresses intermittently after 24 hours to hasten the absorption of the discoloration.
3. Bandage both eyes (Fig. 7-17) and place victim at rest if there is a possibility of hemorrhage within the eye. Hemorrhage within the eye may not be easily seen. The victim may complain of increasing pressure within the eye, and the eyeball may appear to protrude as swelling and discoloration develop.

FEVER

CAUSES: Infection; dehydration; heat stroke; poisoning; vomiting; diarrhea.

TREATMENT:
1. Identify the cause and treat accordingly.
2. Aspirin may be given if tolerated.
3. Cool sponge baths may lower the temperature.

FISHHOOK IMBEDDED IN THE SKIN

TREATMENT:
1. Remove the hook as follows:
   a. To gain some numbness before cutting, place the part in which the hook is caught in stream or lake water to be chilled.
   b. Sterilize a razor blade or sharp knife and cut along the line of hook from barb to shank and remove (Fig.7-21).
   c. If the barbed end is imbedded in deeper tissue, make an incision over the tip of the barb and pass the barb through. Cut the barb close to the skin and pull the remaining hook back out (Fig. 7-22 and 7-23).
2. Clean the wound thoroughly with soap and water, then dry.
3. Apply an antibiotic cream and a dressing.

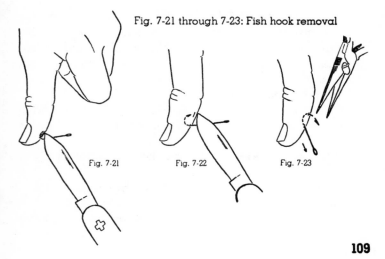

Fig. 7-21 through 7-23: Fish hook removal

Fig. 7-21   Fig. 7-22   Fig. 7-23

4. If signs of an infection develop, seek medical assistance.

FIT

(see Convulsions)

FROSTBITE

(see Cold Injuries)

GUNSHOT WOUNDS

(see also Chest Wounds; Eye Injuries; Chapter 1, "Wounds and Bleeding"; Chapter 5, "Bone and Muscle Injuries")

TREATMENT: The seriousness of the injury will depend upon the size and speed of the bullet as well as the site of entry and exit of the bullet. A rifle shot is more serious than a pistol shot. Also gunshot wounds of the head, chest, and abdomen are potentially more serious than wounds of the arms or legs.

1. Control bleeding (Chapter 1). Hemorrhage may be internal, so watch for signs of shock (Chapter 2). The signs include pale, moist skin; weak, rapid pulse; shallow or rapid respiration, anxiety, and restlessness.
2. Treat for shock (Chapter 2).
3. Cover wound with a sterile dressing. If the wound is in the chest and air is escaping, see Chest Wounds for treatment.
4. If there are signs of internal hemorrhage, apply a cold cloth or ice to the area.
5. Do not give victim anything to eat or drink.
6. Seek medical attention as soon as possible.
7. If gunshot wound is superficial and/or is in the fleshy

parts of the extremities, cleanse with mild soap and water.
8. Cover with a sterile dressing.
9. Medical attention is less urgent in this instance, but tetanus shots and antibiotics will be necessary when medical facilities are reached.

HEAD INJURY

(see Chapter 5, "Bone and Muscle Injuries")

SYMPTOMS: Lethargy; sleepiness; headache; vomiting; confusion; inappropriate speech; blurred or double vision; dizziness; unsteady gait; fever; unequal pupil size; slowing of pulse; marked weakness in arms or legs; unconsciousness; colorless fluid coming from ears or nose.
CAUSES: Blow to head; brain hemorrhage; skull fracture; fall.
TREATMENT:
1. Check for injuries elsewhere and treat in order of priority (see Chapter 2).
2. Maintain absolute rest with head slightly elevated (Fig. 2-2).
3. Place victim on side if vomiting (Fig. 7-24).
4. Maintain open airway (Fig. 3-7).
5. Transport very carefully to medical facility.

Some injuries to the head may not be evident immediately. Be aware that the victim may very gradually develop symptoms, so watch closely fol-

Fig. 7-24: Side-lying position for vomiting

lowing injury and keep victim at rest and observe for symptoms. Awaken every 2 hours, while transporting out or awaiting rescue, to evaluate changes in symptoms, such as the level of responsiveness.

HEADACHE

(see also Migraine)

CAUSES: Altitude sickness; brain tumors; concussions; snow and water glare; fever; allergy; hypertension; infections; migraines; sinusitis; brain hemorrhage; tension; toothache; earache; inhalation of toxic substances

TREATMENT:
1. Determine as best as you can the possible cause, then treat.
2. Quiet, shade, aspirin if not vomiting, and cold compresses to head will relieve most headaches.
3. If persistent seek medical help.

HEART ATTACK

(see also Chest Pain)

SYMPTOMS: Chest pain that may be described as continuous, heavy, constricting, and not relieved by rest; profuse perspiration; moist, clammy skin; paleness; shortness of breath; nausea and vomiting; fainting; very fast or very slow pulse.
CAUSE: Restriction of the blood supply to a portion of the heart.
TREATMENT:
1. Have victim remain quiet in a position of comfort, which is usually a semi-sitting position.
2. Have victim avoid sudden physical effort.
3. Reduce his anxiety by being calm and reassuring.
4. Treat for shock (Chapter 2).

5. Transport as soon as possible to a medical facility.
6. If he becomes unconscious, initiate CPR as necessary (Fig. 3-17).

HEAT CRAMPS

SYMPTOMS: Pale skin; excessive perspiration; abdominal pain; extreme thirst; nausea; dizziness; rapid strong pulse; muscular twitching; severe muscular cramps.
CAUSES: Depletion of body fluids and salt by prolonged excessive sweating; rapid, complete recovery is usual.
TREATMENT:
1. Complete rest in a cool place.
2. Salt is to be consumed in any form, such as salt tablets, a salt solution made up of 1 teaspoon of salt and ½ teaspoon of baking soda in a quart of water, salty crackers, salted peanuts, potato chips, bread and butter liberally sprinkled with salt, or beef jerky.

Do not give alcoholic drinks.
Do not give plain cold drinks.
Do not give stimulants.

PREVENTION: If you are involved in any physical activity in a hot environment, stop and rest for 10 minutes every hour. Try to work or hike during the cooler hours. Drink fluids and replace salt by putting extra in your water. Salt your food more than usual. Wear loose clothing and protect yourself from the sun. Work up gradually to any expected high-temperature exposure.

HEAT EXHAUSTION

SYMPTOMS: Pale, clammy skin; fast, weak pulse; dilated pupils; nausea; vomiting; generalized weakness; coma.
CAUSES: Prolonged exposure to the heat, often with

high humidity; recovery with careful treatment (to prevent heat stroke, which is very dangerous) is usual.

TREATMENT:
1. Move victim to cooler and less humid surroundings.
2. Fan.
3. Loosen clothing.
4. Apply cool compresses to the body.
5. Allow fluids as desired if victim is able to swallow.
6. Encourage the drinking of a salt solution made up of 1 teaspoon of salt (1 salt tablet) and ½ teaspoon of baking soda to a quart of water.

HEAT STROKE

SYMPTOMS: Headache; visual disturbances; hot, flushed dry skin; dizziness; nausea; weak, rapid, and irregular pulse; slow deep respirations; high fever; absence of sweating; muscle cramping; offensive body odor; coma; dilated pupils; convulsions.

CAUSES: Inadequate elimination of body heat due to the breakdown of the sweating mechanism; fatal unless recognized early and treated.

TREATMENT;
1. Immediate reduction of body temperature.
   a. Remove all victim's clothing.
   b. Place him in coolest environment available.
   c. Sponge victim with water, or if near a natural water source, place him in shallow edge.
   d. Allow air to move freely around victim or fan him to increase evaporation and thus cooling of the body.
2. Provide continuous massage toward the heart from the body and extremities to promote circulation of the cooled blood to all parts.
3. Provide respiratory and heart assistance if needed (Chapter 3).
4. Protect victim from self-injury if convulsing, and maintain open airway (fig. 3-7).

5. Hospitalize victim as soon as transportation is possible. Continue cooling methods.
6. Advise victim to avoid immediate reexposure to high heat.

HEMORRHOIDS

SYMPTOMS: Rectal bleeding and pain.
CAUSES: Chronic constipation; chronic diarrhea .
TREATMENT:
1. Sit in warm bath for 30 minutes as often as needed. If you are near a natural hot springs, sit in that.
2. Lie down with feet elevated and apply cold compresses to the rectum if bleeding and severe pain persist. Seek medical attention.
3. Avoid constipation; drink plenty of fluids.

HYPERGLYCEMIA

(see Diabetic Coma)

HYPOGLYCEMIA

(see Insulin Shock)

HYPOTHERMIA

(see Cold Injuries)

OBJECTS IMPALED IN WOUNDS

(see also Chest Wounds; Chapter 1, "Wounds and Bleeding")

TREATMENT:
1. Cut clothing from the area.

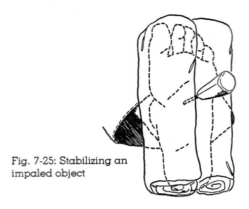

Fig. 7-25: Stabilizing an impaled object

2. Cover with a sterile nonadherent dressing, cut to fit around the object.
3. Immobilize the protruding object with bulky dressings (rolled towels, clothing) so further damage and pain will be avoided (Fig. 7-25).
4. If an extremity is involved, splint it to further reduce movement.
5. Treat for shock (Chapter 2).
6. Transport victim immediately and carefully to medical facility.

Do not attempt to remove the object.

PREVENTION: In general, do not walk barefoot, in or out of water. The feet are the body part most likely to be injured in the wild. There is hardly any wilderness where humans have not preceded you, and broken bottles have a worldwide distribution.

INFECTION

(see Chapter 1, "Wounds and Bleeding")

SYMPTOMS: Pain; swelling; redness; fever; swollen lymph glands; red streaks from wound.
TREATMENT:
1. Rest and elevate the affected part.

2. Apply warm, moist compresses or other improvised bandage to the infected area for 20 minutes at a time.
3. Remove for 20 minutes, then reapply.
4. Repeat until symptoms subside.
5. If symptoms do not subside, then medical attention will be necessary.

INSULIN SHOCK (HYPOGLYCEMIA)

(see also Convulsions; Diabetic Coma)

SYMPTOMS: Hunger; nervousness; weakness; sweating; trembling; faintness; blurred vision; rapid pulse; confusion; unconsciousness; convulsions.

CAUSES: An abnormally low level of sugar in the blood; usually occurs when the diabetic on insulin omits a meal, is vomiting, has unusual activity, or makes an error in insulin dosage.

TREATMENT:
1. If victim is able to swallow, give him orange juice or other fruit juice, or mix 2 – 3 teaspoons of sugar in a glass of water. Hard candy will help if symptoms are noted early enough.
2. If victim is unconscious, check to see if he has a Medic Alert tag or some health identification card, and see if he is carrying an injectable glucose or glucagon. These will reverse the insulin reaction quickly. If not available, place some sugar under his tongue. Then as he regains consciousness, give him the orange juice or sugar water.
3. If there is no glucagon or glucose, transport him quickly to a medical facility.
4. Occasionally the same symptoms may be experienced by someone who is not a diabetic. In these instances, offer the person orange juice at first. This should then be followed by a protein such as cheese, milk, or meat.

PREVENTION: See Diabetic Coma, Prevention.

LIGHTNING

(see also Burns)

SYMPTOMS: Burns at points of contact; weak pulse; irregular breathing; unconsciousness; respiratory and heart failure.

TREATMENT:

1. Start artificial respiration if victim is not breathing (Fig. 3-6 through 3-11).
2. Start CPR if there is no pulse (Fig. 3-17).
3. Resuscitation efforts should be continued for at least four hours unless breathing and heartbeat resume earlier.
4. Keep victim comfortably warm.
5. Treat burns and transport to a medical facility.

PREVENTION: If you are caught in an electrical storm, stay away from the base of trees and remove any metal objects you may be carrying—for example, fishing poles, tent stakes, backpack, and so forth. Get out of and stay away from all bodies of water. Stay clear of isolated trees, rocks, and small shelters, for lightning seeks out lone standing objects. Also avoid the tops of hills or ridges. Ravines, valleys, or dense groves of trees of relatively even heights are comparatively safe. If there is no shelter nearby, the best procedure is to put your feet together and crouch down out in the open and wait for the storm to pass.

LOCKJAW

(see Tetanus)

MIGRAINE

(see also Headache)

SYMPTOMS: Preliminary warning—seeing flashing lights, having double or half vision—may appear several hours before onset; intense throbbing pain in one or both sides of the forehead; nausea and vomiting; blurred vision; irritability; sensitivity to light and sound; constipation or diarrhea; redness and swelling of the eyes.

CAUSE: Unknown.

TREATMENT:

1. Rest in a darkened area until headache goes away.
2. Avoid bending head forward or sudden movements of the head.
3. Aspirin may help if taken very early and accompanied by rest.

MISCARRIAGE

SYMPTOMS: Vaginal bleeding or spotting; mild cramps; passing clots of blood vaginally.

TREATMENT:

1. Provide rest, quiet, and warmth.
2. Keep victim lying down until spotting stops.
3. Anticipate shock (Chapter 2) and obtain medical assistance if bleeding continues or becomes profuse.
4. Bleeding from an early completed miscarriage may be little more than a normal menstrual period and will not require medical assistance.

NOSEBLEED

CAUSES: Spontaneous; injury; hypertension.

TREATMENT: The following treatment refers to a spontaneous nosebleed. If due to an injury, treat like any bleeding wound (Chapter 1). If there is *any* possibility that the nosebleed is associated with or due to a skull fracture, treat as a skull fracture (Chapter 5) and transport victim to medical care immediately (Chapter 7).

1. Sit up to allow drainage.
2. Apply direct pressure by clasping nose firmly between thumb and index finger.

3. Squeeze hard enough to stop bleeding.
4. Breathe through your mouth, and try not to swallow the blood.
5. Continue the pressure for 5 minutes.
6. When bleeding stops, rest quietly in a sitting position and avoid blowing your nose.
7. Ice-cold compresses may be applied to the nose if oozing continues.
8. Sucking on a Popsicle or ice cube will help, especially if it is a child with the nosebleed.

RABIES

(see also Chapter 1, "Wounds and Bleeding"
Chapter 4, "Poisoning")

SYMPTOMS: Can develop within 2 weeks or up to 5 months after the bite; redness, swelling, and pain around the bite area; headache, restlessness, irritability, progressing to convulsions and coma and death from heart failure.

CAUSE: Bite by a rabid animal; children under 12 are more susceptible to being bitten and more sensitive to the infectious saliva of the animal.

TREATMENT: (if it is unlikely the animal is rabid, for example a pet)
1. Cleanse the wound well with soap and water.
2. If wound is deep, do not try to close it with butterfly bandages (see Chapter 8, "First-Aid Kits") or let it be sutured. The wound should be left open to drain.
3. Cover lightly with a sterile dressing.
4. Victim will need a tetanus shot and antibiotics, so seek medical attention.
5. The pet should be turned over to the proper authorities for observation. If the animal has been properly immunized, there is very little chance of rabies developing.

If the animal is wild, it should be killed if possible, and turned over to the authorities for tissue examination for rabies. This is quickly determined and may save the victim painful treatment.

If the animal is not identified or is not located, or if it is determined to be rabid, antirabies treatment must be started.

PREVENTION: Do not attempt to pet or feed any wild animals, no matter how cute or friendly they may appear. Antirabies injections are extremely painful and are not always successful.

SINUSITUS

(see Upper Respiratory Infections)

SMOKE INHALATION
(Respiratory Tract Burn)

(see also "Inhaled Poisons" in Chapter 4)

SYMPTOMS:

   Mild: Sore throat; hoarseness; coughing and sooty sputum.

   Severe: Anxiety; great difficulty in breathing; bluish skin color (cyanosis).

   If unconscious: Look for evidence of burns and swelling in and around the nose and mouth.

CAUSE: Inhalation of hot gases or smoke.

TREATMENT:

1. *Carry* victim to fresh air; walking uses precious oxygen.
2. Loosen all clothing.
3. If there is no head injury, have victim lie down (Fig. 2-1) to allow lungs to drain.
4. Limit intake of fluids.
5. Maintain body temperature.
6. Provide artificial respiration if needed (Chapter 3).
7. Transport to emergency facility.

SNOW BLINDNESS

SYMPTOMS: Gritty feeling in the eyes; burning and redness of eyes; swelling of the eyelids.
CAUSE: Prolonged exposure to sun glare reflected from the snow.
TREATMENT:
1. Lubricate the eyes with a drop of mineral oil.
2. Apply cold compresses.
3. Stay out of the glare until eyes feel better.
4. Wear green-tinted glasses to filter out the ultraviolet rays.

PREVENTION: Wear sunglasses while in the snow.

SORE THROAT

(see Upper Respiratory Infections)

SPLINTERS

TREATMENT:
1. Remove the splinter if possible with a clean tweezer. Pull from the direction that the splinter entered the skin.
2. If unable to remove with the tweezers, sterilize a needle with heat or alcohol. Use the needle to lift up the overlying skin and then remove the splinter.
3. If the splinter is lodged beneath the fingernail, and the end does not extend beyond the end of the

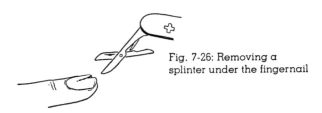

Fig. 7-26: Removing a splinter under the fingernail

nailbed, the nail may have to be split with a sharp scissors and a narrow V-shaped segment cut out to remove the splinter (Fig. 7-26).

4. Apply an antiseptic cream.
5. Apply a sterile dressing or Band-Aid.

STROKE

(see also Unconsciousness; Convulsions)

SYMPTOMS:

Blood Clot or Spasm: Slow onset with episodes of momentary dizziness, loss of balance, weakness in legs and arms, slurred speech; sudden onset with face becoming very red, the mouth pulling to one side, inability to speak, vomiting, collapse, coma.

Brain Hemorrhage: Abrupt onset with a severe headache, dizziness, vomiting, convulsions, unconsciousness, obvious paralysis of one side, unclear speech.

CAUSES: High blood pressure; brain hemorrhage; blood clot or spasm of a blood vessel in the brain.

TREATMENT:

1. If victim is standing, have him lie down and elevate his head and shoulders.
2. If he is unconscious, place him in the side-lying position with the head and shoulders slightly elevated (Fig. 7-24).
3. Loosen all constrictive clothing.
4. Seek medical assistance.
5. Transport him in a lying-down position.

SUNBURN

(see also Heat Exhaustion; Minor Thermal Burns)

SYMPTOMS: Red, painful, swollen skin; if it covers a large area of the body the victim may have blisters, headache, and fever.

TREATMENT:
1. Stay in a cool place.
2. Apply cold, wet compresses for 10 – 15 minutes every hour.
3. Mild analgesic medication such as aspirin may help to relieve pain.
4. If the sunburn is severe, medical treatment may be required.

PREVENTION: Take precautions even on cloudy days, since ultraviolet rays can penetrate the clouds. Protect exposed skin when there is reflection from snow or water. If you are extra sensitive to the rays of the sun, or are on a medication that increases your sensitivity to the sun, use a commercial sunscreen agent, or wear a large hat. Do not stay in the sun for more that 15 minutes at a time if you are sensitive to the sun's rays.

SUNSTROKE

(see Heat Stroke)

TETANUS
(Lockjaw)

SYMPTOMS: Stiffness of the neck and jaw; painful contractions of muscles; convulsions; symptoms may appear as early as four days or as long as three weeks after injury.

CAUSES: Tetanus is a serious complication of any injury if the conditions are right. Tetanus bacteria may be introduced into the body when an injury becomes contaminated with soil, street dust, or animal and human waste.

TREATMENT: The best treatment is prevention by maintaining your immunizations and getting a tetanus injection when you are injured.
1. Cleanse the wound to reduce contamination and possible infection.
2. Cover the wound loosely with a sterile bandage;

change the bandage whenever it becomes soiled or wet.

3. Remove damaged skin or tissue by scrubbing the wound as vigorously as possible with an antiseptic soap and water, and then clip away any small pieces of skin with scissors that have been sterilized with alcohol or flame.

PREVENTION: Maintain your tetanus immunization schedule. It is recommended that a booster be given at least every 10 years. In any case, tetanus shots will be ordered by the physician if the wound is severe, neglected, or untreated and therefore tetanus-prone.

TOOTHACHE

CAUSES: Infection or cavity in a tooth.
TREATMENT:
1. Clean out the food from the mouth and gum area with a warm-water mouthwash.
2. If a cavity is the cause, pack it with a small piece of cotton soaked in oil of cloves.
3. A warm salt-water mouthwash can help reduce pain and swelling.
4. If the cause of the pain is not visible, take a mild analgesic such as aspirin, or hold it in your mouth between your cheek and the tooth.
5. See your dentist as soon as possible upon return home.

UNCONSCIOUSNESS

CAUSES: Since there are many causes of unconsciousness, general emergency measures must be initiated before attempting to determine the cause and to treat more specifically: hemorrhage; shock; head injury; epileptic seizure; poisoning; hyper- or hypothermia; heart attack; severe infections; drug or alcohol overdose; diabetic coma (hyperglycemia); insulin shock (hypoglycemia); stroke; choking.

TREATMENT, GENERAL:
1. Maintain an open airway (Fig. 3-7).
2. Never allow an unconscious victim to remain unattended on his back; his tongue could obstruct the airway or he could vomit and choke.
3. Loosen all tight clothing, such as bras, belts, or collars.
4. Place victim in a side-lying position (Fig. 2-3) only if you are reasonably assured that there is no spinal injury.
5. Control any external bleeding (Chapter 1).
6. Treat for shock (Chapter 2).
7. Maintain body temperature.
8. Assist in breathing and heart massage if necessary (Chapter 3).
9. Check for identifying cards or tags on the victim to assist you in more specific treatment.
10. If unconsciousness continues, transport to the nearest medical facility.

Do not try to make victim sit or stand.
Do not give any food or fluid or medications by mouth.

UPPER RESPIRATORY INFECTIONS

Croup

SYMPTOMS: Occurs in children following an upper respiratory infection; characterized by hoarseness; grunting; fever; apprehension; restlessness; anxiety; bluish skin (cyanosis).

TREATMENT:
1. Provide a warm, humidified environment (Fig. 7-27) by placing a pan of hot water within an enclosed tent, but well away from child.

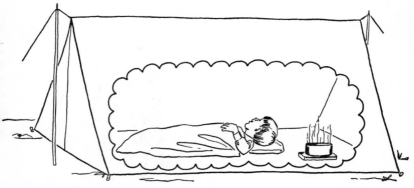

Fig. 7-27: Humidification for croup

2. Transport him to a medical facility if humidity does not relieve the symptoms.

Common Cold

SYMPTOMS: Sore throat; fever; headache; watery eyes and nose; hoarseness; sneezing.
TREATMENT:
1. Avoid chilling.
2. Drink extra liquids.
3. A mild analgesic such as aspirin may be of value.

Sore Throat

SYMPTOMS: Swelling or tenderness between the eye and nose or over the cheek; fever; redness or swelling throat; fever.
TREATMENT:
1. Rest during the fever stage.
2. Salt-water gargles as hot as comfortable and as often as needed.
3. Mild analgesics such as aspirin will give relief from pain.
4. Cough medication may allow rest at night.
5. Drink extra liquids.
6. Avoid harsh-textured foods.

Fig. 7-28: Steam inhalations for sinusitis

Sinusitis

SYMPTOMS: Swelling or tenderness between the eye and nose or over the cheek; fever; redness or swelling around the eyes; bloody or thick and yellow nasal drainage.

TREATMENT:

1. Blow your nose very gently with both nostrils open.
2. Drink plenty of liquids to thin the secretions and promote drainage. Alcohol will aggravate sinusitis.
3. Inhale steam from a pan of hot water (Fig. 7-28). Be careful not to boil the water, as the steam may scald you.
4. Antihistamines may be helpful.

Do not use nonprescriptive nose drops or sprays for more than four days. These will only make your nose stuffier.

VOMITING

CAUSES: Food or water poisoning; ear infections; medications; head injury; heart attack; altitude sickness; migraine; stroke.

TREATMENT:
1. Have victim rest in a quiet place.
2. Encourage deep breathing when nauseated.
3. Check for cause and treat accordingly.
4. When vomiting stops, resume fluids and foods gradually and to tolerance.

WOUNDS

(see Abrasions and Minor Cuts; Chest Wounds; Eye Injuries; Gunshot Wounds; Objects Impaled in Wounds; Chapter 1, "Wounds and Bleeding")

8

First-Aid Kits

You can buy a first-aid kit or you can put one together yourself. In either case, the contents will vary depending upon the individual circumstances of each planned outing. You must consider the length of time you will be away from civilization, the distance to be traveled, the degree of isolation of the area, the climate, the terrain, altitudes, group expertise or lack of it in backpacking and camping, and finally, the ages, number, and states of health of the people involved.

We have organized our first-aid kits into a weekend-outing kit and an extended-trip kit. We feel the supplies for each, as seen in Fig. 8-1 and 8-2, are minimum for a party of four. Below each kit layout we list our suggestions for additions based upon techniques, procedures, and treatment discussed throughout this book.

WEEKEND FIRST-AID KIT

1. Nonadherent gauze pads: two 2-inch and two 4-inch
2. Butterfly bandages: 6
3. Roller gauze or Kling bandage: 1-inch and 2-inch
4. Adhesive tape: 3-inch

5. Band-Aid strips: 8
6. Q-tips: 6
7. Molefoam or moleskin
8. Tweezers and scissors
9. Triangular bandages: 2
10. Safety pins: 4
11. Snakebite kit
12. Signal mirror
13. Lip balm
14. Antibiotic ointment, such as Betadine
15. Hydrogen peroxide
16. Sunscreen agent
17. Insect repellent
18. Oil of cloves
19. Aspirin
20. Salt tablets
21. Cortisone cream

Suggested Additions

- Whistle
- Instant cold pack
- Absorbent cotton
- Antiseptic soap
- Vaseline
- Mineral oil

EXTENDED-TRIP FIRST-AID KIT

1. Nonadherent gauze pads: a box of 2-inch and a box of 4-inch
2. Butterfly bandages: a box
3. Roller gauze: one each of 1-inch, 2-inch, and 3-inch
4. Adhesive tape: 3-inch
5. Band-Aid strips: 16
6. Q-tips: 6
7. Molefoam or moleskin
8. Tweezers and scissors

Fig. 8-1: Weekend first-aid kit

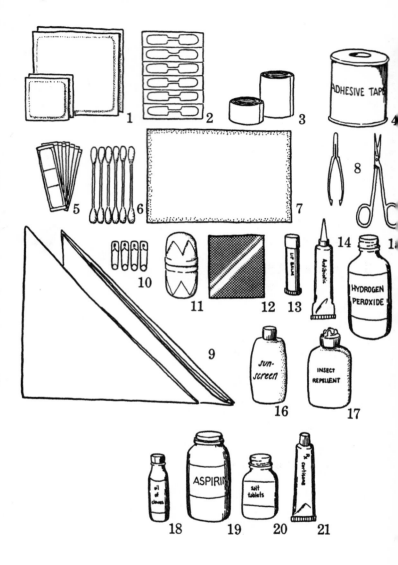

Fig. 8-2: Extended-trip first-aid kit

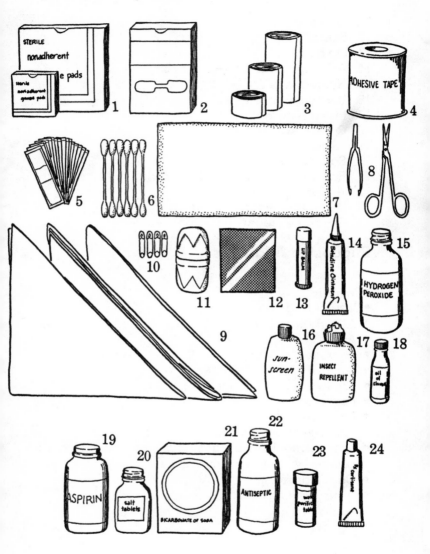

9. Triangular bandages: 3
10. Safety pins: 4
11. Snakebite kit
12. Signal mirror
13. Lip balm
14. Antibiotic ointment, such as Betadine
15. Hydrogen peroxide
16. Sunscreen agent
17. Insect repellent
18. Oil of cloves
19. Aspirin
20. Salt tablets
21. Baking soda (bicarbonate of soda)
22. Antiseptic solution
23. Water purification tablets
24. Cortisone cream

Suggested Additions

- Whistle
- Instant cold pack
- Absorbent cotton
- Antiseptic soap
- Vaseline
- Mineral oil
- Air splints
- Foot powder
- Laxative
- Indigestion pills or liquid
- Antidiarrheal medication, such as Lomotil or Kao-pectate, with doctor's directions
- Cough drops
- Antihistamines

Index

8950